A Year of Programs for Teens

Amy J. Alessio

Kimberly A. Patton

AMERICAN LIBRARY ASSOCIATION

Chicago   2007

While extensive effort has gone into ensuring the reliability
of information appearing in this book, the publisher makes
no warranty, express or implied, on the accuracy or reliability of the information, and does not assume and hereby
disclaims any liability to any person for any loss or damage
caused by errors or omissions in this publication.

Composition in Utopia and Americana using QuarkXpress
5.0 on a PC platform.

Printed on 50-pound white offset, a pH-neutral stock, and
bound in 10-point coated cover stock by McNaughton &
Gunn.

The paper used in this publication meets the minimum
requirements of American National Standard for
Information Sciences—Permanence of Paper for Printed
Library Materials, ANSI Z39.48-1992. ⊂∞⊃

Library of Congress Cataloging-in-Publication Data
Alessio, Amy J.
    A year of programs for teens / Amy J. Alessio,
Kimberly A. Patton.
        p.   cm.
    Includes bibliographical references and index.
    ISBN 0-8389-0903-5
    1. Young adults' libraries—Activity programs—United
States. 2. Libraries and teenagers—United States.
3. Teenagers—Books and reading—United States.
I. Patton, Kimberly A. II. Title.
    Z718.5.A44 2007
    027.62'6—dc22   2006013758

ISBN-10: 0-8389-0903-5
ISBN-13: 978-0-8389-0903-4

Printed in the United States of America

11   10   09   08   5   4   3   2

Contents

Preface

Libraries everywhere offer creative programming for all ages, from infants to seniors. One program does not fit all, of course; libraries need to specialize programming to appeal to specific target groups. Teens need especially exciting and dynamic programs to encourage them to use the public library and its resources. School media centers have the advantage of being age-centered already, but the program options in this book can help make the media center welcoming to teens, and not just for study hall or schoolwork.

There are many good resources for finding ideas for new teen programs, such as electronic discussion lists, books, websites. Events for teens should be offered consistently and continuously and reflect teen desires, celebrations, important reading events, and more. *A Year of Programs for Teens* takes teen services to a new level with step-by-step instructions for planning teen programs. This book also provides stand-alone program and display ideas for building a core teen audience and continuing to attract new participants to programs and to the library.

Good promotion ensures that teens will know about and attend library programs, so most events need to be planned a few months in advance. Using the monthly format of this manual will make program development easier. Planning ahead will also help stretch a budget to cover upcoming events.

Based on the many years of teen programming we have enjoyed, we here outline some of our more successful programs (with a few contributions from some creative librarians whose programs we wish we'd thought of ourselves) in an easy-to-follow format, including tips for gearing a program toward older or younger teens and avoiding pitfalls. Both of us have made our share of programming mistakes and have learned to adapt and work in a variety of circumstances. As trainers for the Young Adult Library Services Association's Serving the Underserved workshop, we have traveled across our states helping library staff at all levels learn to serve teens and enjoy it, and we have learned what other libraries are looking for in terms of new ideas and formats for teen services.

Librarians know that teen programs and services can have immeasurable impact on the lives of young people, but they may need to build a strong case to convince administrators. For example, administrators may be impressed to know that circulation of the Schaumburg Township District Library's teen books has increased 70 percent *each year* since teen programming was developed. Nonetheless, such a result is an added benefit of teen programming, not a reason in and of itself to have that service. Programs designed by and for teens support teen developmental needs. They welcome members of an age group who rarely enjoy such welcomes and let them know that the library is indeed for every person. Today's teens are tomorrow's voters. Enticing them to the library through programming may inspire them in their choices for the future. Losing them sometime between children's story-time programs and adult reading initiatives disserves everyone.

A library's mission statement should specify that the library is a community facility, meaning that all ages may gather there. The mission statement may also emphasize popular materials for all ages. Even a library whose mission statement focuses only on educational materials must market to and program for a range of age groups to ensure that the right user will find the right materials.

Programming for teens recognizes their need for socialization and matches it with library resources. As Patrick Jones puts it in his book *Connecting Young Adults and Libraries* (Neal-Schuman, 1998, 36), "You cannot expect a group of YAs full of energy stored up from a day of school to walk into the library and be perfectly quiet. . . . If your expectations resist flexibility, you are going to create an impossible situation both for you and your YAs."

So let's begin. Or, in the case of many libraries, let's continue the good work already started with teen programs. While some of our ideas, such as teen advisory boards and coffeehouses, are not original, we have worked to provide original twists to make the programs enjoyable for our teens. We hope that readers will find enough ideas to improve teen involvement at their facilities too.

This book begins with steps for developing new teen programming. Next it presents ideas for recurring programs, such as community partnerships, teen advisory boards, and volunteer opportunities. Then it offers in-depth discussions of possible programs for each month of the year, including passive programs (programs that do not require facilitation) and displays. Each chapter includes a list of related resources, and the appendix furnishes useful handouts, forms, and other supplementary materials.

Part One

GETTING STARTED

Overview

PLANNING PROGRAMS

Giving Teens What They Want

Planning teen programming is a lot of work, so why offer programs that teens do not want? You can increase your chance of success by getting input from the teens. Keep in mind that teens' tastes are always changing; the same program offered two years in a row may have vastly different results. Reading teen publications and magazines and tapping into electronic discussion lists (YALSA-L is a great one) will give you a good foundation, but to truly stay on top of teen programming trends, survey local teens about what they want.

To get the best results when creating surveys for teens, include a mix of multiple-choice items and write-in responses. Some people may not bother to respond if a survey seems to require a lot of writing or resembles a classroom assignment. The Teen Program Survey in the appendix provides examples of brief, specific survey questions.

To increase participation, publicize that completed surveys will be used as entries in a raffle. The surveys should be passed out to teens who are already using the library as well as to those who do not. Sending surveys to school media centers, teachers, and community teen centers will help you get responses from teens who rarely use the library. You can also tie your survey campaign to a special event, such as Teen Read Week or National Library Week. See, for example, the National Library Week Teen Magazine Madness survey in the appendix.

Remember that even successful programs can be improved by surveying teens on a regular basis. Post a running survey on your library's website or hand out evaluation forms at each program to get continuous feedback. Always provide space for optional e-mail addresses on survey forms, and make it clear that this information will be used to build a mailing list for promoting upcoming events. Maintenance of such a list should follow library privacy policies, so check how your library handles this.

Working with a teen advisory board (TAB) can be one of the best ways to get ideas for programs and for the rest of teen services. At Schaumburg Township District Library (STDL) in Illinois, the TAB started in 1998 with seven members. These teens began running some youth services programs, such as game nights and story times, then began their own teen events, such as summer scavenger hunts, and grew in influence to the point where the adult library board would not remodel the teen area without their input. The chapter "Making the Most of Your Monthly Teen Clubs" provides detailed ideas for TABs.

Getting Teens in the Door

When teen programming is new and a core group of attendees has not been established, it can be better to have some open events rather than events that require registration. Teens may be shy about signing up at first. Programs without registration can be harder on staff but more effective in attracting teens. For example, if the surveys and TAB indicate that many teens would like to attend a coffeehouse evening, maybe the first ones would be open to all. When attendance begins to outgrow the room, tickets or registration may be required. Registration is also good for events that require a definite count of participants for ordering food or staging a contest. Consider requiring a nominal fee, such as two dollars or five dollars, to ensure that people who register actually come.

Planning the Time and Place

Finding an appropriate location for a teen event involves thinking about many factors. A program that is expected to attract a large crowd or create lots of noise should be held away from high-traffic areas in the library. Some libraries have problems with older teens smoking during breaks in a program. Figure out ahead of time where teens may congregate outside or after the program, and if that will be in a problem area, try to devise a plan for addressing it. Of course teens have rights anywhere in the library, so it is best to try to anticipate every eventuality when planning for a positive outcome.

If a program has to be held in a room with lots of windows, teens may feel too self-conscious to attend. Can windows be covered up with signs advertising what is going on inside? Access to a kitchen may be another major factor in teen programming because food is often involved.

When choosing a date, be sure to look at school calendars to make certain there is no conflict with a major occasion, such as a play, dance, or sporting event. During the summer, it can be good to schedule events for the same day and time each week to build an audience. Having a few programs during the day will attract some younger teens, but having all major events, like band nights and mystery dinners, on Wednesday nights at the same time will help keep teens returning.

The Right Look: Decorating for Events

Have your teen advisers buy the decorations, or select a small, appropriate amount yourself. Oriental Trading, at http://www.oriental.com, is one good place to find inexpensive decorations for many celebrations throughout the year. Local party stores or discount stores are also good sources. For example, a Love Stinks Chocolate Fest will be discussed in the February chapter. STDL used to have a Valentine coffeehouse with lip lights, candy hearts, and heart plates, until the staff realized that this would not appeal to many boys. The next year they switched to an event with black paper goods and everything else upside down, which attracted a much larger audience of boys and girls.

PROMOTING PROGRAMS

Teens need to know all about a program in order to attend. Marketing also involves reaching people who know teens, such as teachers, parents, and church leaders. Specific promotional ideas are discussed for each program in this manual, but there are also some general guidelines that apply to promoting teen events both within and outside the library building.

In the Library

It is very important to promote teen services in-house to library staff. Comprehensive teen services span across youth services, readers' advisory, adult reference, outreach, and more. Attending meetings in other departments to give them a heads-up about a band night or to let them know the many positive effects teen attendance will have on circulation will go a long way toward positive relations. Ask other departments for their input about program ideas or perceived problems to reinforce the idea that everyone in the library is working together for the good of the community. Staff members with teen children are invaluable resources for promoting programs at the library or for ideas about what is popular among teens.

In the Community

Promoting programs to teens does not have to be expensive or hard. Putting a bookmark listing upcoming events in the pockets of teen books either on the shelf or at checkout will market and at the same time indicate which books are going out from the collection. (Books sitting on the shelves for months with the bookmarks still in their pockets are obviously not very popular.) Schools may announce programs over their public address systems. The Fountaindale Public Library in Bolingbrook, Illinois, makes extra-credit coupons listing the names of programs for teachers to hand out, if they choose to do so. Get flyers or posters up in all community agencies or stores where teens congregate. A seasonal newsletter that describes all teen programs for several months may be distributed in the same way. A copy of STDL's teen newsletter, *Teen Happenings*, can be found in the appendix.

Monthly teen programs, such as TAB meetings, may benefit from having youngsters fill out a card with name, address, phone number, birthday (for special promotions), allergies, and the like. These details can be kept on file or in a database for special mailings and emergency contact information. Again, please double-check your library privacy policy for guidelines on maintaining such information.

EXECUTING PROGRAMS

When the day or night of a program arrives, get ready for contingencies. Flexibility is crucial to successful teen programming.

Make certain that you have more than enough staff on hand. Teenagers will probably not be intimidated by you physically, so if a fight or other problem occurs, you will need to have an ample number of adults in attendance to back you up. No one wants serious problems during a fun evening. Access to a phone is important at every event, and staff should plan on carrying two-way radios at larger functions.

Having enough food is another important element of programming. Nothing ruins a program faster than running out of food or beverages. Having enough staff and some extra cash handy can provide a backup option should you unexpectedly run out of provisions. Do not put out all the refreshments at the beginning, either, to ensure that everyone gets some.

You may find yourself answering questions from concerned parents. To make sure parents are not pushing their teens into programs they may not want to attend, it may be a good policy to encourage that telephone or in-person questions about programs come from teens themselves. Promotional materials should indicate clearly that the events are limited to teens. Parents who attend or come in with their teen may make other teens uncomfortable. Exceptions to the teens-only policy may include authors giving presentations, leaders of large groups of attendees, or parents who want to hear their children perform and will leave immediately afterward. No rule should be carved in stone.

Passive Programs

Passive programs are programs that stand alone or that run themselves when you are not around. A good example is the Fall Fashion Fun program for August. Numbered pictures of clothing items from history (such as a corset or a Zoot suit) are photocopied and put on poster board. This display is accompanied by a form containing a list of clothing terms that teens are invited to use to match each numbered picture to its name. As incentive, the names of teens who correctly identify all items could be entered in a raffle for small prizes, or every teen who turns in a form could be given a pencil or other token prize. Such programs could be offered every week in the summer or during school vacations. They are a good way to offer something for teens to do when space and staff time allow for nothing else. They are also a good way to get the attention of shy teens. Forms for each of these programs should be available where teens can easily find them, as well as at service desks where staff interact with a lot of teens. Decorate a box for them to turn these in to, or designate a specific service desk.

USING THIS BOOK The programs outlined in this book could be used in chronological order exactly as described, using the suggested displays and so on. It may be that one program will be a big hit, and teens will be clamoring for the next one. Or perhaps one will not go over well and will need adjustment if repeated in the future. We have learned how to tweak programs to make them work and include suggestions on how you can do the same. For example, maybe a program that we recommend for a particular month here would work better in your community during a different month. This book is intended to be used as a guide or springboard to developing an all-around appealing lineup of programs to showcase the best of what the library has to offer for teens.

Making the Most of Your Monthly Teen Clubs

When librarians build a core group of teens who regularly attend programs, they can interact with them on a deeper level than they could if they only saw them in the library after school. A teen advisory board can come up with a wealth of programming suggestions. Its members are interested in the group or the library itself rather than in attending just one program, and they form relationships with each other and with the library staff. This makes their participation and suggestions even more meaningful and may well attract even more teens to library programs.

When you see what interests your TAB, you can capitalize on your core group before branching out. If teens at your library do not show interest in having an advisory group, find out whether they would take part in a monthly club focused on a topic such as writing or fantasy books or video gaming. Begin by offering something popular like a Dance Dance Revolution (DDR) video game night and poll the attendees about where they would like to go from there for a regular club.

TEEN ADVISORY BOARD MEETINGS

In its simplest form, a TAB is a group of teens who help library staff improve library services to their age group. As it grows, though, it may turn into a large, sustained group that meets regularly. Starting a TAB may be easier than sustaining one and keeping all members entertained. When Amy started a TAB, she had seven regular members. Six years later, she has thirty-five members attending. She found out that teens who attended the TAB meetings were not necessarily coming to other programs, such as the scrapbooking workshops, even when they had helped design them. So she turned TAB meetings into programs by themselves, giving the group a clublike feel. Members still spend time volunteering at library programs and improving library services to teens, but each TAB meeting is a special event for them as well.

The time and frequency of TAB meetings should be chosen by the teens. Some may want to meet every week, but a more likely schedule is every other week or monthly. Some libraries alternate purposes, holding one get-together as a business meeting, then the next as a game night or something like that. Do not expect the TAB to serve as free workers for the library. How many adults would do this consistently with no recognition? Teen advisers need and deserve rewards such as pizza at meetings and bonus coupons for fines. Be sure to include vegetarian and healthy food items, as different teens may have different food requirements or restrictions.

Members should also see the results of their suggestions in a timely manner. After all, they are not teens for long. To reaffirm the importance of the group's input, bring a calendar or list to each meeting indicating the members' suggestions and when the library will act on them.

Plan on building in social time, or members may become too bored or restless to listen to announcements and contribute. Perhaps the first fifteen to twenty minutes of each meeting could be devoted to business, with the rest allotted to a speaker or fun activity.

While members of the library board may not come, it is important to invite them to TAB meetings occasionally so they can see the group in action and know what you are doing. Choose a meeting with a speaker or someone who will positively engage the teens' attention. A TAB representative may want to attend library board meetings as well to keep board members updated on TAB events. It is easier to ask for money or other teen needs when the board is well informed about growing teen services.

Begin each TAB meeting with announcements of accomplishments. Invite the group members to tell others about what they have been doing. Some libraries have officers elected from the TAB, but this could lead to hurt feelings. Putting some teens in charge of projects or events and soliciting people to run programs are good ways to spread the leadership around and still ensure that the teens are the ones running the group. Hiring former TAB members to help with teen programs is another good way to maintain control and provide role models. If former TAB members are going to college in the area, pay them to help with special events. The current TAB members will likely respond better to an older teen than to the librarian. Ideas for TAB meeting activities may be found in the schedule at the end of this chapter.

Teen Writing Club Teens who are not big readers are sometimes creative writers, making their own stories when others' do not satisfy them. When libraries provide author visits, a group of teens will often stay afterward to ask the author questions about writing. If there are a lot of teens in these groups, it may be time to start a teen writing club. Ask the TAB if there is interest in this, and if so, begin hosting writing club meetings immediately before or after TAB meetings to get TAB members to help establish the new club.

There may be someone on the library staff who writes creatively and would like to run the group, or perhaps a local author would be willing to do it for a fee. The Society of Children's Book Writers and Illustrators has a directory of state contacts on their website at http://www.scbwi.org. Teens interested in creative writing are often not interested in publishing their work, though they can be encouraged to do so. They often like to write their feelings down for the sake of doing so. This is a program where a small group is good, as there needs to be time for everyone to share and critique.

It is important to establish consistent guidelines for critique sessions. Specify time limits based on the number of participants. For example, each writer may be given time to read two to three pages of poetry or a story. Before inviting the group to offer criticism, remind them that it is important to say something positive about others' work in addition to giving helpful advice. Make it clear that no negative comments will be tolerated.

A teen writing club can drive other programs at the library in the same way that the advisory board does, but with a different focus. For example, they may run open-mike or coffeehouse nights, or publish writing on the library website or in a print publication. The writing club may also review books for a library newsletter and judge teen writing contests at the library.

Running a teen writing club will involve some icebreakers for the group as a whole before the critiquing begins. Here are some suggestions:

Write Add-on Stories. Have all participants write one sentence of a creative story, then pass their papers to the right. Participants continue adding one sentence and passing papers to the right until all papers have made their way around the group. The originating writers then read the resulting works aloud. In this way, each person gets to add his or her slant to each story.

Create Mad Libs. Mad Libs, a sentence-completion game, will inspire creativity (example: The _____ [noun] checked out a _____ [noun] from the _____ [place]). Mad Libs are always popular, but librarians should be prepared to see themselves portrayed over and over as "person in room." And watch out for those action verbs! Insisting that completed Mad Libs be read aloud will help keep the tone PG-13.

Produce Fan Fiction. Ask members to select a scene from a favorite novel or television show and write a few paragraphs inserting themselves into the action.

Describe an Event. Have members write a description of a memorable event, such as a first kiss, or of something silly, like eating pizza or chocolate.

Write in Rap. After listening to several popular raps played from a CD or read by another group member, participants write their own version of a rap.

Write in Rhyme. Ask club members to write a sappy rhyming love poem. Or ask them to use five words from a Magnetic Poetry Kit or five words on a theme to see if they can work them into rhymes or make them follow a rhythm pattern.

Write Dating Scenarios. Ask club members to write a real or imagined scene that illustrates the best or worst aspects of dating. Possibilities include best or worst ways to ask someone out, best or worst methods to break up with someone, and best or worst places to take someone on a date. (Many are likely to mention the library as a worst place!)

Another good way to encourage teen writing is by offering journals. These could be bought with funds from the library program budget or donations. Inexpensive journals can be purchased from an office supply or discount store. Fancier ones from bookstores or boutiques can be given away as raffle prizes at writing club events or at coffeehouse nights. Journal writers should not have to show their entries to you or to each other.

Coffeehouse Nights

Another good idea for a regular teen program is coffeehouse, or open-mike, nights. Have them at the same time and day each month, like the first Wednesday night or Friday afternoons. Attendance may vary, but chances are good it will build as attendees bring their friends. Be patient because it may take teens a while to learn about these events. Be sure to promote open readings heavily to English teachers, who may give extra credit for participation. Provide a sign-in sheet that asks for e-mail or street addresses to remind teens about future events.

Once coffeehouse nights have a following, it may not be necessary to have a theme or games as ice breakers, but it is always good to have some backup activities on hand. Participants should be encouraged to bring original writing or music to present to the audience, but you may want to keep a supply of skits or poetry books nearby in case people prefer to read someone else's work. Cheesy, outdated skits from books that should have been weeded are a funny way to encourage shy performers. There were many books published about morals or the dangers of drinking in the 1970s that will amuse today's audiences.

Inexpensive snacks, such as soft drinks, chips, and cookies, can be served at coffeehouse nights. Decorations such as simple batik tablecloths, a podium, subdued lighting, and candles can transform a meeting room into a coffeehouse. Ask audience members to snap their fingers after performances instead of clapping, in the traditional manner of 1960s coffeehouses, and the atmosphere will be complete.

The content of the teens' original poetry and writing may be shocking, but it is important not to censor if you want participants to return. If you find that several teens are using excessive amounts of inappropriate language, voice your concerns to them directly and privately instead of applying standards to the entire group. (School libraries will obviously have to follow school codes about this.) In your publicity make it clear that this is a teen event for specific ages or grades and have the event in a meeting room away from the public. If the gathering is going to take place in a public area or in collaboration with another organization, such as a local bookstore or café, try to have it in an area where younger children will not be present.

Many of the icebreakers outlined previously for the teen writing club will also work with small groups at coffeehouse nights. Other suggestions for themes include

Sixties Night. Participants use words from the sixties to make poems while enjoying refreshments typical of that decade. Other decades with matching foods could be featured as well.

Friendship Night. Participants make friendship bracelets using the supplies on their table.

Skit Night. Volunteers present skits using published TV script books or by creating scenes from popular shows or cartoons.

Whose Line Is It Anyway? Use games from the television show or its website, including having volunteers speak only in questions or song titles.

Scary- or Horror-Theme Night. At STDL, a Little Coffee Shop of Horrors is held each year in October during Teen Read Week. Typical coffeehouse activities, such as poetry reading, can be given a horror theme with the presentation of Poe's "The Raven" and other scary classics. (See the October chapter for more details.)

Karaoke Night. Karaoke Nights can be hard on staff, but they are fun for teens. Participants may sing along with a karaoke machine or dance and sing with Karaoke DDR. Encouraging group performances and awarding small prizes to all participants will promote a positive spirit. You may need to remind teens that this is not *American Idol.*

Some of these themed events, such as Karaoke Night, may become new regular programs. Offering regular teen programming will establish an audience and help develop ideas for new programs at the library.

SCHEDULE FOR TEEN ADVISORY BOARD MEETINGS

There are many publications written about teen advisory groups. Several are listed at the end of this chapter. Instead of going over the nuts and bolts of TABs, we suggest the following ideas for what to do with the groups throughout the year.

January

Be careful about scheduling the TAB meeting so it does not conflict with finals for high schoolers. It is likely that attendance will be low this month in any case, with papers being due, sports activities, and the like.

Elvis's Birthday. Amy is a huge fan of the King, so at one January meeting, teens were served fried chicken and Krispy Kreme donuts. Some made their own grilled peanut butter and banana sandwiches. Then they listened to Elvis music and watched short clips from two Elvis feature films and his 1968 TV special. A short Elvis trivia contest completed the hour.

Martin Luther King Jr.'s Birthday. The more important King with a birthday in January can be celebrated by having teens watch taped excerpts from his speeches. Prepare scenarios of acts of racism as they may occur in the teens' lives, and have volunteers act out possible solutions. Create scrambled lists of laws promoting racism and segregation and the years they were created and see if teens can correctly match each law with its date. These ideas would also work well for Black History Month in February.

February

Anniversary Party. Amy's TAB celebrates their anniversary each year in February. The teens have to list their all-time favorite TAB activity and plan for future activities. Staff set out photos of highlights from past years.

Mardi Gras or Love Stinks. These programs are described in depth later in this work and could easily be adapted for this month's TAB meeting.

March

Pre-prom Scare or Internet Safety. A lot of teen tragedies occur in the spring in conjunction with end-of-the-year events. This is a good month to discuss teen drinking, drugs, or Internet safety. Invite a speaker from the local police force or a state's attorney. One speaker at Amy's TAB listed the costs of being arrested for driving under the influence, then divided the total by the average teen's hourly wage to show how long it would take to pay for such poor judgment. Be sure that the activities and speakers are relevant, or the teens may tune them out.

Job Skills. During the spring teens begin thinking about summer jobs. Take this opportunity to review interviewing and job skills with them. Go over employment applications from the library and other places in the community where teens may want to work, and answer questions teens may have. Invite a speaker to discuss interviewing or have a library administrator interview a few teens as a demonstration. Be sure to show what a bad interview looks like, too! Go over phone and in-person customer service as well.

April

Scrapbooking. As teens start thinking about graduation and similar events, find a local artist, research the topic yourself, or ask one of the teens to demonstrate how to make a scrapbook. Bring in an instant or digital camera and take pictures of graduates for a poster in the teen center or for a display on TAB activities. Members can make picture frames at this event too. Raffle a photo album to participants.

Speak Only in Rhyme. For poetry month, have a game or length of time during which teens can speak only in rhyme.

National Library Week Librarian Legends. Do teens really know the library? Make up some library legends, mix them with some unusual facts, and see if teens can tell them apart. Example: Last month one patron checked out 250 items at once.

May

Cinco de Mayo or Other Ethnic Food Festival. May is a good time to introduce teens to Mexican culture. Serve Mexican foods, such as make-your-own tacos and churros; break open a piñata; and teach a few useful Spanish phrases. See how many teens can carry on a lengthy conversation in Spanish. These ideas can be carried over to other ethnic festivals, such as Asian, Italian, or Middle Eastern, with appropriate foods and language discussions.

Graduation Party. Say good-bye to departing high school seniors and congratulations to eighth-grade graduates at this event. Have the high school TAB members write up advice for the eighth graders, and invite the seniors to discuss their future plans with the group. Have a cake and special mementos for the graduates. Consider passing around yearbooks from other generations (perhaps ones kept at the library) to let participants laugh at hairstyles, messages, and the like. Invite students to bring their own yearbooks so other TAB members may sign them.

June

Lock-In. During a lock-in, teens stay in the library after hours or when the library is closed. A lock-in may run for a few hours, or even all night, which may make staff nervous. The first time you have a lock-in it is a good idea to limit registration to TAB members, teens who are known to staff and are familiar with each other. For a long program with lots of activities, more staff may be needed than usual. This program gives teens a chance to explore the library with activities such as scavenger hunts and to bond as a group.

Pizza Tasting or Barbecue. Get a pizza from a number of local establishments and have teens vote on a favorite. Another, cheaper way to do this is to buy and vote on various brands of frozen pizza. The summer is also a good time to have a barbecue or outdoor meeting.

July

Healthy Eating. Prepare a salad bar or other healthy fare for teens. Have participants make fruit smoothies with yogurt or their own trail mix. Prepare a list of popular fast foods and see if teens can identify which are the healthiest and which contain the most fat, sugar, or calories.

August   *Vacation Meeting.* Meet outdoors and have s'mores and nonalcoholic beach drinks. Set up a volleyball net or other activity for the group.

September   *Program Planning.* Have teens work in teams to list three of the worst library program ideas they could possibly think up. Then have them exchange lists with another team and figure out how to fix the programs so people would attend. This is a great way to brainstorm. Or, list library problems, such as vandalism or budget cuts, and see what ideas teens come up with for fixing them.

October   *Halloween Event.* Invite teens to make their own English muffin pizzas, but dye the cheese green or blue beforehand for creepy effects. Play Ghost instead of Bingo. Have a mummy wrap, with teams competing to wrap a member in toilet paper. The team that uses the entire roll without breaking it and within the allotted time is the winner. Invite participants to make disgusting desserts by decorating brownies or to create scary pumpkins. Present a demonstration of weird makeup. Have teens identify items by sticking their hands in boxes of strange-feeling objects, such as grapes and ricotta cheese.

Make a Difference Day. List agencies that have needs for specific items such as food or clothing and have the TAB members vote on which to help. Then have them design a program to follow through. A book drive is another good way to help. Or, invite teens to bring a can of food to the meeting to help a local food pantry prepare for the upcoming holidays.

November   *Holiday Cards.* TAB members can create holiday cards for themselves or others. Or perhaps local hospitals or nursing homes could use holiday cheer. Bring out creative Ellison die-cut shapes and other sources of inspiration.

December   *Holiday Event.* Have a white elephant gift exchange for TAB members with things they have brought from home. Then give them all a small real present to show your appreciation of their work for the library. Teens may also bring in a new, good gift for someone in the area who might not otherwise receive one. (Many religious organizations and villages have gift drives for families in need, but often they do not get enough gifts for teens.) Introduce mancala for Kwanzaa and the dreidel game or potato pancakes for Hanukkah, and have teens make crackers with cardboard tubes, wrapping paper, and small candies. Invite them to talk about family traditions. Other project ideas for this meeting are making gingerbread houses or decorating cookies.

RESOURCES ABOUT TEEN ADVISORY BOARDS

Teen Advisory Group Site: http://www.ala.org/ala/yalsa/tags/tags.htm. The Young Adult Library Services Association has a website dedicated to teen advisory groups. The site includes articles on starting such groups, activities for keeping them going, and interviews with groups across the country.

Tuccillo, Diane. *Library Teen Advisory Groups*. Lanham, MD: Rowman and Littlefield, 2004.

Community Networking

As programs become more popular and a core group of teens is established, attendance may outstrip budget and time constraints. Perhaps the crowd is getting too large for the library meeting room. Or maybe the same really troubled teens come to the coffeehouse each time and read poetry about how they want to kill themselves. These are not issues one is trained to deal with in library school.

It is time to call in experts, and there are probably several community agencies that can help with these issues. Partnering with local agencies is a win-win proposition for expanding the resources and reach of the library. Partnering can allow libraries to host larger programs at other locations; to have police attend programs on occasion; to establish a network of professionals to call if a teen issue is beyond what can be handled at the library; to pool resources, especially in times of shrinking budgets; and to get the word out about library services. For example, when popular stores are included in promotions, they are more likely to donate prizes and provide places to put flyers in the community.

Choosing agencies to work with is simple enough. Where are the teens in your community? Obviously, they are at the schools, which are essential partners. Also, they are at the YMCA, parks, counseling centers, retail outlets, religion-sponsored youth groups, scouts, and the like. What are the most popular social venues? Does the park district have junior high dances? Do the malls have back-to-school fashion shows? Do the counseling centers have support groups or trips for teens? If you are not up-to-date on what the community is doing for teens, begin contacting the different agencies to find out.

The next step is to introduce yourself to the people who work with teens in your community. This can be done by hosting a function to which all agencies will be invited, such as a luncheon or tea, or by visiting each place to meet and talk to staff. Members of the community, including reporters who have supported teens, should be invited to a TAB event, such as a holiday party, as a thank you. The teens and the adults will both enjoy this and it will reinforce the positive partnerships.

A good first project for a community network is to compile and distribute a directory of agencies that serve teens in the area. It could list the addresses, hours, and contact information of teen drop-in centers or the dates and times of popular teen programs. It would also include information about regular library teen programs and the website where information on teen programs can be found. The directory can be compiled on a website, through the library, with links to each agency. A bulletin board devoted to community teen events is another easy way to continue partnerships, as is setting up a table at teen events. For example, have a table in the school cafeteria during Teen Read Week to promote a library card drive or contests, or set up a booth at a teen dance or event at a mall or park.

Amy Alessio started the Schaumburg Township NETwork for Teens through STDL when several students in her teen advisory board had problems that she did not know how to address. Some were involved in serious theft and vandalism, some were drinking heavily, and one tried to commit suicide, twice. There is no group of teens that does not include individuals with some problems or issues, and it is helpful to be able to talk to counselors and other agencies as needed. For example, at STDL, the police began coming to TAB meetings to facilitate positive discussions about drugs and alcohol. The staff at one counseling center provided training for youth services and teen personnel at the library in how to defuse fights. Other agencies involved in the network include the local mall, the YMCA, the park districts, counseling centers, schools, and the local community college.

Depending on their expertise, staff from the agencies go to different places to run programs. For example, librarian Amy Alessio has done jewelry design at the girls' club at one counseling center and taught origami at the YMCA and area teen centers. A police detective ran a popular mystery dinner at STDL. And when one teen center had a fire, the other agencies pitched in to donate computers and game tables, host events, and even place staff at workstations.

The network meets bimonthly to go over what each agency is doing and what kinds of problems they are encountering. They jointly put out surveys about teen programming to reach as many teens as possible. All groups put each other's program flyers up at their facilities, too. Many are different colors or have coupons for tracking what is being picked up where. Not only has this increased visibility for teen services in the community, but it has also helped reduce duplication of services and competition among the agencies for dates and types of programs.

VOLUNTEERS AND COMMUNITY SERVICE PROJECTS

Teens will need to volunteer at the library or do unpaid work for a variety of reasons, including graduation or church requirements, interest in library work, or community service prescribed by a court of law. All three are valid, important reasons, and it is good public relations for libraries to cooperate with local agencies in helping teens with such needs. While working with volunteers of any age can involve problems, working with teens can be among the most rewarding aspects of your job. In fact, this may be your only opportunity to engage some teens and show them what the library has to offer.

Teens who have broken the law and who are required to perform community service at the library provide a librarian with an opportunity to make a big difference in their lives. It is a mistake for libraries to single this group out by placing lots of unnecessary restrictions on their work. In our experience, they are often better behaved than teens who are required to do hours for graduation from high school, because they know it is a crucial chance for them to clear their records (depending on local laws). It is also an important chance for the library to work with local law-enforcement officials. Too often this agency is overlooked by librarians as an opportunity for partnership. The police should know what services are available to teens through the library and know the staff members who work with teens. Contact with the police should not be limited to phone calls when there are incidents at the library. Developing a relationship with the police can lead to interesting speakers for teen groups, tours of the police station, and more. This will improve the way teens see police and the way the police see teens. When we see our teens having problems, our well-established relationship with the police has also enabled us to ask for advice without giving names. When some members of Amy's TAB were dealing with substance abuse, she invited the police to come speak to them. The officers came several times, to demonstrate drug-sniffing K-9s, to talk about party pitfalls, to discuss backing away, and to offer tips on Internet safety. The teens listened to their messages and were able to develop positive relationships with the officers, who returned to present additional programs over the years. The police department DARE program then invited the TAB to make a short movie about what the library has to offer teens. The movie was filmed at a library lock-in with a digital video camera, and was edited by village officials who were also members of the NETwork for Teens. It was four minutes demonstrating in a humorous way what people thought the library was like, then what it actually was like, including a montage of teens having fun at the library. It was shown to all sixth-grade classes for several years.

Teens who need to fulfill community service requirements should be viewed differently from adults in that category. Often, the teens' crimes do not involve threats to other people as, for example, an adult's drunk driving might. A positive, respectful relationship with a librarian could make an important difference in a teen's behavior.

If it is a policy at your library not to work with community service teens, consider a change. Very few adults could honestly say they never broke a law when they were teens, and many of today's teens assigned to community service have been caught shoplifting or committing similar minor offenses. Perhaps worried library administrators could agree to work with teens who have been found guilty of nonviolent offenses. Sometimes teens who have broken the law are bored and looking for attention in ways that could be channeled into productive work at the library. We have hired some teens to work for pay at the library when their community service was completed.

Basic Tenets for Volunteers

There are some basic rules for working with volunteers of any age, and some special considerations for teens performing community service.

To ensure clear communication, teens should be expected to sign a contract that outlines the library's guidelines. If a teen then creates problems, perhaps by not showing up or by doing sloppy work, the contract will clearly outline the consequences. In the case of community service teens, it is understood that the police will be contacted if there are problems. A sample contract for teen volunteers is provided in the appendix.

Staff should be informed about the importance of volunteers and how their work makes everyone else's work easier. It is a good idea to remind staff that because most volunteers will have had little training in librarianship, they are apt to make mistakes and that those mistakes should be met with tolerance. Also remind staff of the important role that volunteers play in maintaining relationships with religious organizations, schools, and police. Under no circumstances should the staff be told what community service teens have done to break the law. Only the person working directly with such a teen, and possibly administration, needs to be informed about this. When a new volunteer begins, be sure that staff receive a memo encouraging them to be welcoming. Recognize that some staff will never be agreeable to working with teen volunteers—of any kind—and find ways to schedule so that their time with teens is limited.

It is important to let all volunteers know that their work is needed at the library and why. Community service teens in particular should feel that they are engaged in something that contributes to the business of the library. They can and should be assigned some low-skill tasks, such as labeling and sorting donations, as long as such work is tempered with variety and practical job training.

Volunteers and community service teens should be given rewards for good service. Some free time now and then, some fine-clearing coupons, or other library-related bonuses will leave all volunteers feeling good about their library experience. Many facilities have reward luncheons or pizza parties for long-term volunteers.

Tried-and-True Volunteer Projects

The key to happy volunteers is to assign them projects that match their skills. To help in making assignments, you may wish to have your volunteers fill out a questionnaire about their skills during their orientation.

For example, an artistic teen may enjoy doing displays, and a computer-skilled community service teen might be perfectly suited to maintaining the public computers and helping patrons solve computer-related problems.

Teens should always have more projects than they have time for, with a clear indication of priority. This way, if staff is busy and cannot help them, they can work quietly on something else instead of interrupting every five minutes to ask what to do next. Providing them with both basic tasks to perform every time they come in and some special projects helps avoid the problem. For example, print out all the current best books or pages from journals and have teens search the catalog to find out which titles the library does not yet own. Or have them straighten a specific area of the library each time they come in.

Volunteers are often helpful in running youth craft programs or teen programs. They can also help with reading program sign-up. Community service teens clearly need to find places to spend their time constructively. If they enjoy helping you run some teen programs, they may continue coming after their service is done.

Teen volunteers can bring good perspective to making book lists for their own age group, either from computer research or from their own interests. They can also fill and design displays as well as do some basic shelving, depending on their training.

Engaging Teen Volunteers

As more and more school media centers have their funding cut, fewer and fewer young people learn library skills. Teen volunteers have a good opportunity to acquire a few basic skills. Consider designing a simple scavenger hunt that introduces teens to various service desks and areas of the library.

All teens volunteering in the library should have a full tour of the facility, and even of branches where possible. If an audio tour is available, this should be utilized on the first day of work as part of orientation. You will be surprised at how many areas of service teens are unaware of. (Think about what adult patrons do not know!)

Then volunteers should be instructed in the finer points of the work they will be doing. This should involve time spent observing staff at different service points and behind the scenes. Asking your volunteers to interview three different staff members is another good way to help them understand library work. Some teens may be put off from becoming a librarian by hearing about the required master's degree, but their interest may be piqued once they've talked to a computer staff member, a graphic artist, and another paraprofessional.

Design an exercise that requires teens to compare amounts of time spent searching the Internet versus searching a reference book. Ask them to use standard reference works to answer some basic reference questions, such as who invented something, what happened in a certain year, or who wrote the lyrics for a song. Then ask them to perform an Internet search to find similar information, such as three sites that back up a certain fact or a significant year in the history of the town. Be sure to include links available right on the library's website and to incorporate electronic reference products and serial searches. Teens will be surprised at how quickly they can utilize the reference materials as opposed to the Internet in many cases.

High school teens should be thinking about their futures. Community service teens may not previously have had a great deal of positive guidance about career choices. Take this opportunity to help them. Some libraries offer career training and skills workshops for community service teens. Even teens required to fulfill service requirements for graduation may not have had previous opportunities to learn basic job skills.

Ask all volunteers to fill out a job application for the library. Critique their responses and tell them where they could improve, if needed. For example, many teens do not realize that their computer skills are highly marketable, as is knowledge of a foreign language. Then have someone on the library staff interview them and offer tips. Discuss customer service rules with them and invite them to serve some patrons with staff nearby. Other good areas to explore are phone and e-mail etiquette.

Allow teens to spend some of their volunteer hours researching career possibilities. They could do self-tests such as Myers-Briggs, either from books or online, to look at their strengths. After they have a few answers about their interests, encourage them to research three schools that offer classes for at least two career choices. Make sure they investigate local colleges. Provide them with a form they can use to record and compare information about tuition, fees, admission requirements, titles of courses that interest them, and the like. If time allows, they may even be able to use library resources to practice writing a personal statement.

Many high school teens do not have the time or inclination to read for pleasure. Counter this by allowing volunteers to spend a few hours doing some pleasure reading. Or require the teens to select some nonfiction materials related to a hobby and read them. You could also provide the titles of some powerful teen fiction or nonfiction that highlights what happens to teens who get in serious trouble, such as Walter Dean Myers's *Monster*.

These types of activities raise the level of interaction between staff and volunteers above the labeling, time-killing activities some libraries use to a meaningful experience for everyone involved. Teens who have a good experience volunteering at the library, no matter the reason for their being there, should be able to depend on library staff to supply positive references for work or school in the future.

OTHER PARTNERSHIPS IN ACTION

Cosponsored Events

For both Halloween and St. Patrick's Day/Mardi Gras, teens in Schaumburg Township have been invited to large dances hosted by several agencies. With several agencies contributing funds, the events include food, DJs or bands, contests, and nice prizes. Also, they are held in places with gymnasiums or pools for the teens to use. These are events that the library could never host by itself.

When several agencies pool resources like this, it is important to spell out who is responsible for each facet, including decorations, staff, prizes, food, publicity, and monies donated. Some agencies may not be able to contribute as much money as others, but all can put in time soliciting donations, setting up the location, and so forth.

Tournaments

Instead of taking your TAB bowling or to play mini-golf, why not have a tournament with another agency? Keep it a simple, fun, one-day activity. After the main competition is completed, continue the fun by inviting the teams to exchange members so that each team includes representatives from both organizations, either coed or boys against girls. If there are intramural sports in your area, consider having your TAB participate as another way for members to interact with a variety of other teens.

Working Together to Help Others

Consider hosting a teen food drive across the agencies in your community network. To add incentive, the library could offer to accept food in place of fines. Perhaps the agency that collects the most food for a local food pantry would win a pizza party or similar reward. November and April are good times to do this kind of program. It may be helpful to find out what the food pantry is most looking for, such as ingredients for holiday meals or paper goods that are not covered by food stamps.

Teen Invasion

One year the Schaumburg Township NETwork for Teens combined efforts to provide teens with fun and diverse summer activities. Each agency came up with things for teens to do, such as taking classes, finishing the summer reading program at the library, going to museums, volunteering with seniors and at day-care centers, and attending outdoor concerts. Teens earned points for participating in the activities, and those who earned twenty-five points by the end of the summer were eligible for raffles, with prizes that included $500 gift certificates to malls for back-to-school clothing. Afterward, an essay contest encouraged teens to write evaluations of the program for a chance to win a college savings bond. Each agency hosting the summer events contributed toward the prizes.

During the next few summers, the program was streamlined to make it easier for teens. Instead of awarding large prizes at the end of the summer, the network presented smaller gift certificates of $25 and $50 at four drawings spaced throughout the summer. Teens turned in tickets after each activity, and the drawings were cumulative. Therefore, teens who turned in tickets early in the summer had entries in all four drawings. The essay contest was eliminated in favor of a survey, and a separate drawing was held for teens who turned in their responses on the survey. As a result of these changes, each agency saw an increase in teen attendance at their programs, giving Teen Invasion an overall increase in participation of 30 percent each year. A sample promotional flyer for the Teen Invasion can be found in the appendix.

■ ■ ■

Teens, especially younger ones with limited transportation, may not know what the library has to offer. A teen who needs help in some way, especially for a serious or threatening issue, may not know where to get it. Every partnership the library is involved with increases the chances of engaging such teens.

Part Two

A YEAR OF PROGRAMS

January

January can be cold and dreary in many parts of the country, and many people feel some letdown after the festivities of the holidays and the New Year. For high school teens, there is the stress of finals looming ahead. Days off from school and snow days could mean more business than usual at the library as teens prepare for assignments and crucial tests. During January it is important to honor Martin Luther King Jr.'s birthday. Other events that lend themselves to displays and programming include Elvis's birthday on January 8, Super Bowl Sunday, Presidents' Day, and Abraham Lincoln's and George Washington's birthdays.

Finals Study Break

High school teens will already be in the library studying for finals. School systems often designate a day off before finals begin, and that day or a weekend day are optimal times to offer a study break. Having this program in a drop-in format will make it fun and easy to attend. It will be one of the easiest and most appreciated programs offered for teens!

PREPARATION TIME	15 minutes plus shopping time
LENGTH OF PROGRAM	2–4 hours (drop-in format)
NUMBER OF TEENS	20–25
SUGGESTED AGE RANGE	Grades 9–12

SHOPPING LIST   Food: vegetable tray and dip, chips, pretzels, soda,
　　　　　　　　　　　　　　lemonade, cookies

　　　　　　　　　　　Music and a portable CD player

　　　　　　　　　　　Raffle box and tickets

　　　　　　　　　　　Raffle prizes such as video rental coupons or coffee
　　　　　　　　　　　　　shop gift certificates

　　　　　　　　　　　Mad Libs, mancala, darts, and other simple, fast games
　　　　　　　　　　　　　for small groups of teens

SETUP

**Two Weeks
before Program**

Advertising ahead of time can be done at the schools. Send fun, bold posters to school media centers and ask administrators to add the event to public announcements. Consider sending coupons to classrooms ahead of time that will entitle the bearer to a bonus raffle ticket at the program.

Day of Program

Tables in a meeting room or section of the library where food is allowed can be set up with snacks and games. A table near the door should be stocked with raffle tickets and a box for them. Comfortable chairs and/or lounging pillows will add to the relaxed atmosphere.

　　　A raffle for some stress-breaking activity, like renting a movie or getting a treat at a coffee shop, will add to the theme. The raffle tickets should include a box that teens can check if they want information about future programs sent to them. This will turn a simple program into a lasting investment.

MAKE IT HAPPEN

At this time of year, high school teens will be totally focused on finals and may not have read the library calendar. To make sure teens know about this program, ask if an invitation to attend can be announced over the library's public address system at the beginning of the program and halfway through. Circulate through the library after the program has started and personally invite teens who are studying to attend.

　　　A study break program is almost as easy as a passive program. Simply set out the food, games, and raffle slips, and let the teens drop in. Do not put all the food out at once, but add items as the attendance grows. Some teens may go back out in the library to get their friends, so supplies will need to last. Difficulty in predicting the amount of refreshments needed is one disadvantage of a drop-in program.

　　　You may find that some extra teen incentives, such as pens and key chains, have been lurking in closets. Put these in a box and let students choose one before filling out a raffle slip for more prizes. A raffle should have a few guidelines. Each teen should be allowed to enter only once. Exceptions may be made if raffle tickets take the form of book reviews or if bonus raffle tickets have been awarded to teens in recognition of special service or achievements. If teens are allowed to enter only once, it may be a good idea to have staff surreptitiously check the entries for duplicate names before the drawing begins. Or have students hand staff the slips and have staff put the slips in the box. Names could be drawn every fifteen minutes to half hour, depending on the prizes. Prizes could be anything from gift certificates to mugs to hot chocolate packets to help with late night studying. Large candy bars are another inexpensive favorite.

Giveaways are always a draw, and the simpler the better. If a few prizes are left over from previous months, put them in a box and let raffle winners reach in and get one. Many teens who attend study breaks may not be regulars, so they will not have seen the prizes before. They may laugh at their winnings, but they are likely keep them and use them. Inexpensive prizes for this kind of grab bag may include finals-related items like novelty erasers, pencils, and pens.

Variation   This kind of program can easily be offered for junior high students on a day off from school, but perhaps with the focus on board games and prizes for winners. Members of this age group may not be as concerned and stressed about time and may be looking for something to do.

The snacks could have a theme that will appeal to both junior and senior high students, if both will be attending, like a hot chocolate bar where participants can create their own beverages with various flavors of cocoa, sprinkles, whipped cream, and mints. This can be done with instant hot chocolate and warm milk or hot water in thermoses if the refreshment room is not attached to a kitchen.

Warm Up with a Good Book

The holidays have passed, finals are over, and a new semester has begun. Keep teens using the library and reading for fun and relaxation with a scaled-down, low-cost reading program.

PREPARATION TIME   3 hours

LENGTH OF PROGRAM   4–8 weeks

NUMBER OF TEENS   Probably no more than 100

SUGGESTED AGE RANGE   11–18 years

SHOPPING LIST   As prizes for teens who finish the program, purchase or solicit gift certificates and coupons for hot beverages, mugs, cookies and snacks, gloves, hats, mittens, and other items that fit the theme of warming up. Depending on the level of participation, the total cost to run this program will vary from free if all prizes are donated to $150 if prizes are purchased.

SETUP

Two Weeks before Program

Make snowflakes by folding and cutting 8½" × 11" pieces of white construction or copy paper. Decorate them with glitter or glitter glue and mount them in the library.

Prepare a winter reading log with space for readers to record their name, address, age, school, titles read, authors' names, and brief reviews. (A sample reading log for Warm Up with a Good Book is included in the appendix.) Make a generous number of copies of the log and leave them on tables, shelf ends, and display spaces in the teen area.

MAKE IT HAPPEN

The goal for program participants is to read three books or listen to three audio books between January 1 and March 31 and to supply the information requested in the winter reading log, including a short review of each book. Teens who complete their logs and return them to the library then qualify to enter a drawing for prizes.

Variations and Helpful Hints

Instead of focusing on books, keep track of pages read or time spent reading.

Solicit donations for prizes and coupons from area merchants.

Use leftover coupons and prizes from the summer reading program.

Have prizes of various values. For example, give everyone a small prize, like a free hot chocolate, and then draw for one grand prize.

Instead of using preprinted reading logs, have teens bring in lists of books they have recently read. Encourage teens to bring in their favorite title and present it to other teens in the library.

This is a good opportunity to promote booklists. Compose your own on different themes, from African American fiction to books on the arts. Any theme will do. Leave the lists around the library, on tables, and so forth. Also recommend books from the following lists of award winners from the Young Adult Library Services Association:

- Alex Awards (titles written for adults with young adult appeal): http://www.ala.org/ala/yalsa/booklistsawards/alexawards/alexawards.htm
- Best Books for Young Adults: http://www.ala.org/ala/yalsa/booklistsawards/bestbooksya/bestbooksyoung.htm
- Michael L. Printz Award for Excellence in Young Adult Literature: http://www.ala.org/yalsa/printz/
- Outstanding Books for the College Bound: http://www.ala.org/ala/yalsa/booklistsawards/outstandingbooks/outstandingbooks.htm
- Popular Paperbacks for Young Adults: http://www.ala.org/ala/yalsa/booklistsawards/popularpaperback/popularpaperbacks.htm

- Quick Picks for Reluctant Young Adult Readers: http://www.ala.org/ala/yalsa/booklistsawards/quickpicks/quickpicksreluctant.htm
- Teens' Top Ten Books (titles chosen by teens): http://www.ala.org/ala/yalsa/teenreading/teenstopten/teenstopten.htm

For further variations, make a "Staff Picks" display and have each staff member recommend his or her favorite book for teens.

Teen Job/College Fair

Teens may not realize that their first job does not have to be in retail or fast-food, though many may enjoy the discounts and flexibility of such work. Teens can also find meaningful work that they enjoy and that will help them develop skills and interests they can pursue into college. The library is a good forum for introducing teens to local employers and college representatives. Organizing a job and college fair also promotes community networking.

PREPARATION TIME 6 hours

LENGTH OF PROGRAM 2–4 hours

NUMBER OF TEENS Up to 200

SUGGESTED AGE RANGE Grades 10–12, or ages 15–18 years

SHOPPING LIST
Food: cookies, punch, ice
Tablecloths, napkins, plates, cups
Small gift bags or donated grocery bags
Pens and pencils
Name tags
Donated items for door prizes and giveaways
Refreshments and supplies will cost about $100 (per 100 attendees)

SETUP

At Least Three Months before Program

Contact the city personnel office, the Chamber of Commerce, and area merchants who hire young people from fourteen to eighteen years old to work in their businesses. Invite them to send representatives or printed materials, including job applications, to the event. Include someone from a local personnel agency or human resources department to conduct practice interviews so teens can get hands-on résumé and interviewing tips. Also invite area vocational schools and training centers as well as local colleges.

Day of Program   Set up tables around the perimeter of the room and assign each participating business or school one table to use for display. In a separate room or corner, arrange an area for mock interviews. It should include a video camera, TV/VCR, small table, desk, and two chairs. Stuff small bags with name tags, pencils, and pens. Set out and arrange refreshments.

MAKE IT HAPPEN   Kick off the program with a short presentation of résumé-writing and interview tips by an expert from a personnel agency or human resources department. If possible, include skits that illustrate both good and bad interview techniques. Examples of bad interviews are always a hit with teens, and they are an effective way to highlight potential mistakes. After the talk is over, teens will have time to travel from table to table, talking to the various representatives and practicing mock interviews. It may help to provide evaluation forms for both teens and agency representatives to find out which types of jobs and educational training the teens were most interested in and if there is a topic they would like to hear a speaker discuss in the next year's program.

Variations and Helpful Hints   Invite a representative from a local vocational or business school to give a short talk on noncollege options.

Invite volunteer organizations to participate by encouraging teens to volunteer in the community as a way to prepare to enter the job force.

JANUARY PASSIVE PROGRAMS

Crazy New Year's Resolutions. Create forms on which teens can write five crazy New Year's resolutions. Encourage creativity. No "do better in school" or "get in shape" resolutions allowed here!

Ten Ways to Avoid Studying for Finals. Create one-page forms with one paragraph explaining how high schoolers can design a list of ten creative ways to avoid studying for finals, or, for junior high teens, ten creative ways to avoid studying of any kind. Be sure to post the lists in the teen area or online so that other teens can enjoy reading them.

JANUARY RESOURCES

School Stress

Bloor, Edward. *Story Time*. Orlando, FL: Harcourt, 2004.

Cappo, Nan Willard. *Cheating Lessons*. New York: Atheneum Books for Young Readers, 2002.

Cobb, Katie. *Happenings*. New York: HarperCollins, 2002.

Crutcher, Chris. *Whale Talk*. New York: Greenwillow, 2001.

Duncan, Lois. *Killing Mr. Griffin*. Boston: Little, Brown, 1978.

Nelson, Blake. *The New Rules of High School*. New York: Viking, 2003.

Oates, Joyce Carol. *Big Mouth and Ugly Girl*. New York: HarperCollins, 2002.

Sheldon, Dyan. *My Perfect Life*. Cambridge, MA: Candlewick, 2002.

Wolff, Virginia Euwer. *True Believer*. New York: Atheneum Books for Young Readers, 2001.

Display Ideas
Squeezable stress balls, large stacks of school books, alarm clocks, empty bottles of Tylenol

February

February starts wintry and ends with thoughts of spring. Even this short month provides great programming opportunities. Remember to keep teen interests in mind: Valentine's Day will not attract many teens to a program, but a Love Stinks Chocolate Fest just might. Teens outside of Louisiana may not be familiar with the fun of Mardi Gras and will enjoy being exposed to the traditional New Orleans celebration. February is also Black History Month and a great opportunity to provide programming in honor of African American culture.

Love Stinks Chocolate Fest

A traditional Valentine's Day party will not attract many teens, especially not males, but a Love Stinks Chocolate Fest that pokes fun at some of the mushy, commercialized aspects of the traditional holiday allows teens to participate in enjoyable—and delicious—games. What teen (or adult for that matter) does not like chocolate? Valentine's Day brings lots of interesting candies to the stores, and teens will enjoy this opportunity to sample some and to play with different forms. (Ever heard of chocolate plastic?) Many different activity ideas are provided here. Choose three or four favorites for a two-hour program.

PREPARATION TIME	45 minutes plus shopping time
LENGTH OF PROGRAM	2 hours
NUMBER OF TEENS	20–40

SUGGESTED AGE RANGE	Grades 5–10
SHOPPING LIST	Hot chocolate and water

For additional items, see the recipes in the "Make It Happen" section.

SETUP
Day
of Program

Valentine decorations can be used for the fest, but with a twist. Paper hearts can be made into broken hearts by drawing jagged lines on them or cutting them in two. Cute Valentine lights or cutouts may be hung upside-down around the room. Combine Halloween decorations with some Valentine's Day items. For example, a cute, heart-covered Cupid could have a little rubber skeleton or spider on his arrow. Black table-cloths or paper products mixed in with anything red lends the right tone for this program. Foil-covered Valentine's candies can be scattered on tables surrounded by four to six chairs. On each table have a large chocolate kiss as a centerpiece along with a fondue pot.

MAKE IT HAPPEN
Chocolate Plastic

Chocolate plastic is a confection used by pastry chefs to make roses and other decorations for fancy cakes. It can also be used by teens to make cool shapes to play with (think play-dough for teens). Here is a very simple recipe we modified from one the real chefs use. You will need

1 12-ounce bag of semisweet chocolate chips

$^2/_3$ cup of corn syrup

Powdered sugar if needed

Melt chocolate chips in a double boiler or microwave. Stir in the corn syrup until smooth. Refrigerate at least three hours. Knead a little to see if the dough is workable. If it is too sticky, work in a little powdered sugar. Tear off golf-ball-size chunks and place in cupcake cups (one for each teen). Have fun with cookie cutters, rolling pins, or whatever the teens like to make fun shapes. If the chocolate starts getting sticky after awhile, the teens can eat it.

Chocolate Tasting

Set out a variety of chocolates in various forms for tasting, such as

White chocolate chips or squares

Milk chocolate chips, squares, hearts, or other shapes (Hershey's kisses will work well)

Semisweet chocolate chips or squares (Dove dark chocolate squares work well)

Bittersweet chocolate chips or squares (Baker's chocolate, cut in half)

Unsweetened chocolate chips or squares

Chocolate Fondue   You will need

> Fondue pots and Sterno or mini Crock Pots; one big pot or several small ones
>
> Wooden skewers (the kind used for shish kabobs); large wooden toothpicks would also work
>
> Apple slices, orange slices, banana slices, strawberries, pretzels, pineapple chunks, large marshmallows, angel food cake cut into 1-inch chunks
>
> Semisweet chocolate chips—1 cup for each small fondue pot
>
> Whipping cream—½ cup for each small fondue pot

Small pots can be set up at individual tables, with six to eight kids per table. This will provide a cozier setting. Keep an eye on the Sterno; sometimes it gets a little too hot. Melt chocolate chips in the fondue pot, add whipping cream, and mix well. Once the chips are melted, put the lid halfway on until it's time to start eating. Using skewers, dip fruit, cake, and marshmallows, as preferred. Eating fondue will be a new experience for most participants, so remind them of a few points of etiquette: no double dipping, politely share the fruit and cake with others, and so forth. Or the fondue can be spooned onto paper plates so that party goers can dip from their own plates.

Sappiest Love Poem   You will need

> Scratch paper and pencils
>
> Examples of bad love poetry, especially the rhyming type, from books in the collection

Read aloud, or ask teens to read, some of the bad poetry from the collection. Invite teens to write a couplet that must rhyme and be appropriately sappy. Telling them in advance that they will be expected to read their poems aloud will help to avoid especially crude words or sentiments. Or if the group is shy, offer a little incentive, like a candy bar or pencil, to those who will read aloud.

Another option is to have teens write unromantic poetry, using words from a magnetic poetry kit or words provided on cards.

Romance Writing   You will need

> Scratch paper and pencils
>
> Made-up romance Mad Libs–type game

Have teens work with partners to fill in words in a Mad Libs passage from a romance novel. To create such a passage, take a few paragraphs from any romance novel and copy them into a computer. Then omit some nouns, verbs, and names, and replace them with write-on lines. Try to avoid using "Part of Body," though there will be many opportunities to do so in most romance novel passages. Teens may read results aloud if time allows.

Mancala with M&Ms   You will need

M&Ms

Empty egg cartons, one per pair of teen players

Mancala is an old stone game that originated in Africa. The object of the game is to collect as many stones as possible in one's collector pit (mancala). The board consists of twelve playing pits (six pits by two pits) plus one large collector pit at each end. Each player owns the six playing pits on his side of the board and the large collector pit on his right. If playing with egg cartons, players can collect their stones in a pile at the end of the carton. Players start with three stones in each playing pit. Player 1 takes all the stones out of one of his pits and puts one in the next pit to the right, one in the second pit to the right, and one in the third pit to the right. If Player 1 reaches his own collector pit, he drops a stone into it, and that stone is out of play. (Players put stones in their own end pit but not in their opponent's pit.) Player 2 then takes all the stones out of one of her pits and distributes them in the same way. Players take turns moving counterclockwise around the board. If the last stone in a player's hand is placed in the collector pit, that player gets another turn. If the last stone in a player's hand is placed in an empty pit, that player takes the stones from the opposite pit and places them in his collector pit. The game continues until all six pits on one side of the board are empty. At that point, both players count the stones in their collector pits, and the one with the most stones wins.

Mancala is even more fun with M&Ms as the playing pieces. You will need thirty-six M&Ms, preferably in Valentine colors, per mancala board. Players may not eat playing pieces until the game is over.

There are many variations in mancala. Typing *mancala rules* in any search engine will bring up Internet sites with rules. One site that lists a few variations, with clear instructions and illustrations, can be found at http://www.centralconnector.com/GAMES/mancala.html.

Heartbreakers   You will need

Scratch paper and pencils

Ask teens to work in small groups to create lists on one or more of the following topics: Ten Worst Ways to Break Up with Someone, Ten Worst Ways to Ask Someone Out, or Ten Worst Places to Go on a Date (be prepared to hear that the library is one of these!). If time permits, let groups read some items from their lists aloud.

Variation   To make the Love Stinks program appeal to older teens, offer a few of the activities in a coffeehouse format. For example, Heartbreakers, Chocolate Fondue, or mancala could be interspersed with traditional open-mike events.

Mardi Gras Outside of Louisiana!

The flavor of Mardi Gras is achievable even up North! Introduce teens to the traditions and foods of the famous New Orleans festival. Consider making this event into a fund-raiser to help rebuild New Orleans by asking teens for a small donation or charging a nominal entry fee that will be contributed to a Hurricane Katrina fund or a large agency such as the American Red Cross.

PREPARATION TIME 1 hour plus shopping time

LENGTH OF PROGRAM 1 hour

NUMBER OF TEENS 20

SUGGESTED AGE RANGE Grades 7–12

SHOPPING LIST Mardi Gras beads

Chocolate coins

Piñata

Packaged biscuit dough; colored sprinkles in purple, green, gold; small plastic baby

(A purchased king cake may be substituted for the above baking supplies. The king cake is a circular coffeecake, often with cream filling on the inside, that is decorated with wide bands of purple, green, and gold sugar. A small plastic baby is hidden inside the cake or included to tuck into a piece when cutting.)

Black or colored half masks or masks cut from foam or card stock

Feathers

Stick-on jewels

Crown

If a meal is desired, fried chicken and red beans and rice are good choices for the theme.

SETUP

Day of Program

Yellow or gold, green, and purple tablecloths may be used for tables, with four to six chairs apiece. Sprinkle gold coins (foil-covered chocolate coins) liberally on the tables. Put masks and beads up on the walls to continue the theme. Hang a themed piñata in a large space.

MAKE IT HAPPEN   Let teens pick one strand of beads as they walk in the door; either green, gold, or purple.

King Cakes   If an oven is available, have teens make mini king cakes by forming biscuit dough in circles. They can decorate them with the sprinkles. Lags of time while the mini king cakes are baking can be a problem. Have teens form teams by bead color—purple, gold, green—for a trivia contest, or have them list all the words that can be made from MARDI GRAS while they are waiting. Or simply have them make their masks during this time. While the cakes are cooling from the oven, secretly hide the plastic baby in one. The teen who gets that cake will be the King and gets to wear the crown and be the first to try the piñata. (If a king cake is purchased, the teen who eats the piece with the baby hidden in it will be the King.)

Mask Making   Teens can make Mardi Gras masks with the feathers and jewels. Glitter glue is another easy way to jazz masks up. If participants are uncomfortable about wearing the masks, ask them to create masks as decorations for the teen center of the library or for the children's area.

Piñata   If the king has not broken the piñata open, to earn a turn to hit it, teens must do something such as put on a mask, or mention a recently read book, or say a word in French from a prepared list. The piñata should be filled with more chocolate coins.

The piñata event can get a little crazy if there is not enough space. Teens may pretend piñatas are for little kids, but as soon as they get a chance to hit one, they may get carried away. Be prepared. It is a good idea to use a broom instead of a bat in case someone misses badly. Make other teens stay behind a line. Breaking the piñata a little beforehand will ensure that this event will not continue for too long.

Black History Month:
Traveling the Underground Railroad

A good way to honor black history is through a program on the Underground Railroad. States west of the Mississippi River may have local sites from the railroad that can be highlighted during the program. While there is debate about how quilts were used in the Underground Railroad, the topic can introduce discussion and spark interest in history as the teens create their own quilt. This program could also be held in November for Veterans Day, tied in with the Civil War.

PREPARATION TIME	30 minutes
LENGTH OF PROGRAM	3 hours, allowing for individual sewing time
NUMBER OF TEENS	50 maximum
SUGGESTED AGE RANGE	Grades 5–12
SHOPPING LIST	Fabric
	Sewing needles
	Scissors

SETUP

One Week before Program

Choose three or four simple quilt blocks from the resources listed at the end of the February section—that is, blocks with few pieces and in the shapes of squares or rectangles—and make several photocopies of each pattern.

Cut fabric into nine-inch blocks. This is an easy size to cut into smaller pieces and will show teens what the finished size should look like.

Cut out the pieces for a block to use for demonstration during the program.

MAKE IT HAPPEN

Quilting in the Civil War

Some aspects of the Underground Railroad translate well into vivid activities for teens. There is some debate about whether or not quilts were used to signal that a house was part of the Underground Railroad. Find out if someone at a local quilt or fabric shop could come to talk about the history of quilts during the Civil War and could teach teens to hand sew a simple block from that era. If no one is available, there are several good references with patterns you can use to prepare a presentation yourself. Barbara Brackman is an expert in Civil War–era quilts. Two of her books, *Quilts from the Civil War* and *Civil War Women*, have projects to try. The fictional book *The Runaway Quilt* especially discusses the debate about signals, as do other titles by Jennifer Chiaverini. The main character in *The Runaway Quilt* discovers a quilt and tracks down its history.

Take one of the photocopied patterns, such as Flying Geese or Log Cabin, and cut it into the required pieces. Pin those pieces onto fabric and cut out the resulting shapes. Invite teens to begin sewing the pieces together by hand. Note: Four-sided pieces are easier to sew together than triangles. Triangles stretch while sewing, so let teens know they have to make small stitches. By the time teens have sewn a block, they will have a new appreciation for the crafts from the Civil War period.

Teens should have time to browse the books that show the quilt patterns from that time period. Consider providing graph paper and colored pencils so that teens may design their own "code quilt blocks" that mean something important to them. If time permits and teens are good at the sewing, one of those blocks may be blown up on the copier and transferred into a pattern, then cut from fabric pieces and sewn.

Living Historians   Another way to make discussion of the Underground Railroad interesting to teens is by inviting a historical reenactor to speak for a one- to two-hour program. Civil War reenactors are available in every state east of the Mississippi River and some are available in the West. Many units of Civil War reenactors have websites that may be found by entering the name of a state and "Civil War" in a search engine. Reenactors love any excuse to put on their period clothes and discuss the 1860s. Teens will find the hands-on artifacts and clothing more impressive than book illustrations. Some schools and libraries may have regulations about weapons on the property, so be certain to check on that before the speaker arrives.

FEBRUARY PASSIVE PROGRAMS

Love Stinks Song Lyrics. Invite teens to write their own terrible rhyming love songs. Provide a list of words to start them off, or perhaps make a display with a rhyming dictionary and lists of song lyrics.

Candy Heart Slogans. Use a die-cutter, such as an Ellison machine, or ask volunteers to cut out three-inch hearts from colored paper. Staple or tape the hearts to a bulletin board along with two simple rules: (1) teens are invited to make up candy-heart slogans of seven letters or less and write them on the hearts, and (2) names are not allowed to appear on the hearts. If language is a concern, add lines on the back of each heart that must be filled out with the slogan writer's name and phone number. (This can be done by typing labels and sticking them on the back.) Teens that turn in a heart slogan could receive a candy heart or a small package of candy hearts to make it fun.

Celebrate Black History Month. Create a poster of famous black entertainers and ask teens to list the entertainers' names and what they did to become famous.

FEBRUARY RESOURCES

**Love Stinks
Chocolate Fest**

Allenbaugh, Kay. *Chocolate for a Teen's Heart*. New York: Fireside, 2001.

Brenner, Joel. *The Emperors of Chocolate*. New York: Broadway, 2004.

Coe, Sophie. *The True History of Chocolate*. New York: Thames and Hudson, 1996.

Cormier, Robert. *The Chocolate War*. New York: Pantheon, 1974.

Dahl, Roald. *Charlie and the Chocolate Factory*. New York: Penguin, 1964.

Fluke, Joanne. *The Chocolate Chip Cookie Murder*. New York: Kensington, 2000.

Klause, Annette Curtis. *Blood and Chocolate*. New York: Delacorte, 1997.

Murfitt, Janice. *Chocolate: Over 100 Irresistible Chocolate Ideas*. Boston: Little, Brown, 1989.

Wrede, Patricia. *Sorcery and Cecilia*. Orlando, FL: Harcourt, 2003.

> *Display Ideas*
> Lids from empty heart-shaped chocolate boxes cut in jagged broken hearts, hearts cut out of black paper, upside-down hearts

Mardi Gras

Bannos, John. *The Heaven on Seven Cookbook*. Berkeley, CA: Ten Speed Press, 2001.

Landau, Elaine. *Mardi Gras: Parades, Costumes, and Parties*. Berkeley Heights, NJ: Enslow, 2002.

Lindahl, Carl. *Cajun Mardi Gras Masks*. Jackson: University Press of Mississippi, 1997.

MacMillan, Dianne. *Mardi Gras*. Berkeley Heights, NJ: Enslow, 1997.

Mitchell, Reid. *All on a Mardi Gras Day*. Cambridge, MA: Harvard University Press, 1995.

Smith, Julie. *New Orleans Mourning* (Skip Langdon series). New York: St. Martin's, 1990.

> *Display Ideas*
> Mardi Gras masks, beads, crowns, feathers

Civil War Quilts and the Underground Railroad

Brackman, Barbara. *Civil War Women*. Lafayette, CA: C and T, 2000.

———. *Quilts from the Civil War*. Lafayette, CA: C and T, 1997.

Chiaverini, Jennifer. *The Runaway Quilt*. New York: Simon and Schuster, 2002.

Civil War Fiction

Alphin, Elaine Marie. *Ghost Soldier*. New York: Henry Holt, 2001.

Ernst, Kathleen. *Ghosts of Vicksburg*. Shippensburg, PA: White Mane Kids, 2003.

Forstchen, William R. *We Look Like Men of War*. New York: Forge, 2001.

Hite, Sid. *Stick and Whittle*. New York: Scholastic, 2000.

Peck, Richard. *The River between Us*. New York: Dial, 2003.

Rinaldi, Ann. *Girl in Blue*. New York: Scholastic, 2001.

> *Display Ideas*
> American flags, Civil War doll clothes, canteen, quilt squares

March

Spring is rapidly approaching, and that means spring fever for teens! Lots of important events will have their attention at this time of year, from graduations to concerts, banquets, and prom. Sadly, this is also a time for lots of drinking, parties, and emotion. Program planning for March should help keep teens more engaged and informed than ever. It is a good idea to host a spring break program or two for those who are not lucky enough to travel somewhere warm. The programs suggested for spring break offer a choice of drop-in events. A Who's Sorry Now? Bored Game Tournament gives teens a chance to explore board- or video-gaming skills. Women's History Month offers another opportunity for a theme program, while a program about health and relaxation can provide a refreshing change of pace.

Spring Break Ideas

Some lucky teens will be able to go somewhere warm for spring break, but chances are that many will be hanging around the library, especially the younger teens. To take advantage of this, consider planning drop-in programs that are easy and fun. Often teens have big assignments for school and will stop by programs for only a little while. Spring break is also a good time to recruit teens for summer events.

Planning an elaborate program for this week may be futile if many teens will be away. The programs below keep it easy and fun. Some of the programs outlined elsewhere in this book, such as the Finals Study Break, would work well for spring break, as would drop-in craft demonstrations as part of the Knitting Club or Origami programs.

Clean-Out-the-Closet Craft Day	A spring cleaning of teen supplies will make space for summer events. Take odds and ends of crafts and put them out on a first-come, first-served basis until they are gone. This works well with supplies for beading, scrapbooking, rubber stamping, card making, T-shirt painting, and the like. If there are no good supplies left in the teen area, consider clearing out some of the youth services supplies and using them in projects for older kids. For example, use gemstones for notebook decorating.
Cooking Demonstrations	Plan cooking or tasting demonstrations for a couple of hours. Have different types of chocolate or cheese for fondues. (Ingredients can be heated in a microwave if fondue pots are unavailable.) Or have a healthy sandwich-making bar with different types of bread and fillings. A make-it-yourself bar can also be done with different syrups and toppings for coffees, teas, and hot chocolates.
Friendship Bracelets	Making friendship bracelets is a simple drop-in program that works best with younger teens. To ensure simplicity, supplies should be limited to safety pins and embroidery floss, but beads can be added as well. Teens may know how to make some version of these already—ask one of your regulars to teach the procedure if you do not know it yourself.
Movie Marathon	In preparation for the Movie Marathon, choose a group of recent movies (if you have a performance license) and let teens vote on which ones they would like to see. Three movies is a good number for a marathon, and emphasize in publicity and on the day of the event that teens may come and go as they please. You can choose movies on a theme, such as superhero movies, sequels, school, or scary movies, but be sure that advertising makes it clear that this is a teen event and that PG-13 movies may be shown. At the marathon, have different flavors of popcorn, such as caramel, cheese, and no butter, or have the supplies for teens to add their own flavors to plain popcorn.
Virtual Hawaii	If teens cannot travel, bring the tropics to them. Show a movie set in Hawaii, such as *Blue Crush*. Give teens leis when they walk in the door and have regional food, such as nonalcoholic piña coladas, coconut, and pineapple. Have Hawaiian music playing when they enter the room. To make this program more elaborate, add a hired hula demonstration.

Who's Sorry Now? Bored Game Tournament

Lots of bored teens hanging around the library? Advertise a board game tournament. This can be competitive play among many players of the same game or a drop-in event with periodic prizes. Easy and inexpensive, this is great program for days off from school or as a regular feature during the summer. Fancier versions of this include video gaming on the Internet, DDR, and events where teens can drop in and bring their own equipment and games.

PREPARATION TIME 30 minutes

LENGTH OF PROGRAM 2–3 hours

NUMBER OF TEENS For competitive play, the number of players will be determined by the game. For example, a Sorry tournament would call for multiples of four players, with the limit based upon how many boards are available. For drop-in programs, there is no limit.

SUGGESTED AGE RANGE Grades 6–12

SHOPPING LIST Board games—multiple copies of one game for competitive play

Food: cookies, pretzels, chips, and similar snacks

Simple prizes such as books, novelties, candy bars, small gift certificates

Raffle slips and box, if desired

SETUP

Day of Program Set up stations or tables for each game with chairs, a bowl of snacks, and all the game pieces in working order. If scratch paper and rules are needed, have those at each site also. If multiple teams have signed up for competitive play, organize a seating chart of players.

MAKE IT HAPPEN

Competitive Play To have a game tournament, publicize which games will be played and at what time the event will start and end. If it is a Sorry tournament, for example, start a game as soon as four players arrive. If there is an odd number of teens, add staff players to round the group out. Only teens should move on to the next round, unless staff is once again needed to round out a group. If a staff member wins, the teen closest to winning at that table should be declared the winner. To arrive at a champion, the winning teens from each table could play each other until one teen remains. If time is an issue, it is possible to award a small prize to the winner at each table. To fill time while teens are waiting for their round or after they have been eliminated, set up other games for noncompetitive play. Invite participants to enter a raffle as well so that even a teen who is eliminated early can still win a prize.

Drop-in Play	Set up stations with favorites games, such as Sorry, Life, and Monopoly. Also put out checkers, mancala, and chess in case there are two players wanting to play a game by themselves. Put a bowl of snacks at each table. Have periodic drawings for prizes among attendees.
	Regularly scheduled board game tournaments make a great summer drop-in program. An event such as Monday Madness, where games and snacks are available from one o'clock to four o'clock each Monday afternoon in July may grow to be a hit.
Variations *Chess Club*	Chess clubs are becoming popular again. Test the waters for establishing a chess club in your area by offering a chess tournament. Teens should register ahead of time so that you can match opponents as closely as possible by age. Have timers and a book of rules handy, and because this could be a long event for teens who lose early, award prizes at the end of each round to maintain interest.
Theme-Based Games	Choose a theme for games, such as the Lord of the Rings or the Simpsons. Themed versions are available for traditional games, such as Monopoly or Risk, with adapted boards and playing pieces. For example, Simpsons Clue has a poisoned doughnut as a weapon. Another theme idea is kiddie games, such as Candyland and Chutes and Ladders, for humor or nostalgia.
Design-a-Game	Supply sheets of poster board, construction paper, glue sticks, and markers and have teens design their own games. Some die-cut companies, such as Ellison, have pieces for this kind of project in kit form.

Women in History Fashion Show

A program entitled "Women's History Month Celebration" will probably not bring teens running. However, a women's fashion show with historical costumes and a discussion of etiquette and rules for women during several eras in our country's history, possibly titled "Time Travel Fashion Show," may prove of interest. Fashion illustrates the society in which women lived. For example, flapper outfits showed the freedom enjoyed during the 1920s, and Victorian clothing expressed great modesty. The evolution over time of underwear alone, besides being interesting and fun to observe, illustrates women's increasing freedoms. The program could consist of famous women wearing the fashions of their times and discussing their lives and their roles. Models might include the woman's suffragist Susan B. Anthony in the late-nineteenth century, Louisa May Alcott in Civil War times, or Betsy Ross in the Revolutionary War era.

Although the preparations are elaborate, this program is fun for all involved. Consider making it into a fund-raiser for teen services by charging a registration fee.

PREPARATION TIME	20 hours
LENGTH OF PROGRAM	2 hours
NUMBER OF TEENS	Up to 25 models and 75 audience members
SUGGESTED AGE RANGE	Grades 7–12 or mothers and their daughters in grades 5–9
SHOPPING LIST	Tea or punch fixings
	Historically accurate cookies or cakes, depending on the costumes; for example, for the Depression era, serve sugarless items

SETUP **Two Months before Program**	This program is elaborate, so it is a good idea to form a committee to organize it or to host it with a partner agency, possibly a school or arts center. If you decide to use a committee, ask teen advisory board members to serve or advertise for volunteers to begin meeting at least two months in advance. Committee members could be responsible for contacting agencies about costumes, publicity, modeling, and narration during the event, as well as helping to serve the food. Volunteers from a partner agency could also help with those tasks.

It may be easiest to obtain costumes from different time periods from local theaters or high school theater departments. The fashions that you can find will help you decide which women to portray in the show.

Contact the Society for Creative Anachronism (http://www.sca.org) to find local reenactors who might be willing to donate their services or costumes for the show.

Create a log of borrowed costumes and accessories and which teens are wearing which items. Be sure that models know the procedure for turning items in after the show so that all can be returned to the proper owners.

Large department stores sometimes offer etiquette workshops. Presenters of such workshops could be invited to contribute to the program, or library staff can research old norms for young ladies that seem preposterous today, such as never showing the ankle.

A script that presents a few facts about each outfit, including who donated it for the event, should be created for a narrator to read on the day of the event. The script should also provide background about each era presented and mention some famous women from that period. The narration could be read either over softly playing period music as each outfit is modeled or before the music is played, as a series of longer introductions at the beginning of each era of outfits. Several volunteers could take turns reading, or a single narrator, perhaps a library staff member, could read the entire script.

One Month before Program　Research, rehearsals, and fittings will take a couple of weeks. The research will focus on the eras that match the available costumes and appropriate refreshments. Music from each era represented will also be needed to play while models display the corresponding clothes. Members of the TAB or regulars at the library could be the models for this program. Models should practice walking in their complete costumes at least once. Plan on one dress rehearsal with all models in costume to practice cues, music, and narration.

One Day before Program　Decide whether your meeting room lends itself more to a stage-based presentation or can accommodate a simple runway among the tables. Either setup will require a modeling area and a place where audience members can sit and admire the fashions while enjoying refreshments. If possible, set up the stage or runway in advance to verify that its design will work.

　　Use the log that you made earlier to make sure that the costumes are in order and labeled by model. Check that all accessories are with each outfit. Also check that all necessary music is available, that the audio equipment is in good order, and that the person in charge of music knows how to work the equipment.

Day of Program　Ask models to arrive one to two hours before the program. Have a volunteer check in all models as they enter. Make sure that a volunteer who is able to sew, either adult or teen, is on hand to help with last-minute problems as models get dressed.

MAKE IT HAPPEN　If refreshments will be served before the show, have some models in costume greet audience members as they arrive and show them where to sit and where to find drinks and cookies.

　　When the audience is settled and ready to view the fashions, be sure to announce all sponsors and donations. Then turn the show over to the narrator. After the show, if there is enough clothing, it may be fun to dress up volunteers from the audience. For example, women's fashions at the time of the Civil War required several layers of underwear, which could be placed over the clothing of a volunteer to show how long it took to get dressed.

Feeling Good: Yoga and Smoothies

Contributed by Rose Allen,
Teen Librarian, Mount Prospect
Library, Mount Prospect, Illinois

Yoga and smoothies are positive health trends that teens will enjoy. This program could simply be about smoothies if no one is available to demonstrate yoga, but the two combined are sure to attract some new aficionados. At this program, teens will be invited to concoct a delicious, low-fat smoothie with fruit variations after a one- to two-hour yoga demonstration.

PREPARATION TIME

2 hours

LENGTH OF PROGRAM

1½–2¾ hours

NUMBER OF TEENS

25

SUGGESTED AGE RANGE

Grades 7–12

SHOPPING LIST

Food: bananas, strawberries, mangoes, melon, oranges, peaches, pineapple, milk, soymilk (for vegan teens), yogurt (vanilla works best, but include soy yogurt, too), ice

Tablecloths, napkins, cups, spoons

SETUP

Two Months before Program

Contact an individual who is proficient in yoga who will have a good rapport with teens. When the program is advertised, emphasize that each participant should bring a mat. If any staff members have been yoga students, solicit their talent to keep cost down.

Two Hours before Program

Cutting up the fruit takes time, so try to allow at least one to two hours of prep time. Employ the assistance of another staff member or two because the bowls of fruit will have to be replenished continuously. Placing blenders on four to six tables away from the ingredients table will create mixing stations that ease congestion, so you may need to solicit staff to bring in blenders or buy some ahead of time. After each smoothie is prepared, the blender will have to be washed, so this activity will run more smoothly if there are at least two assistants. Depending on the size of the room and the preference of the yoga instructor, a limit may have to be placed on registration.

Set up tables around the perimeter of the room. Place the cut fruit, yogurt, milk, ice, and cups on one long table, and place a blender on at least four to six smaller tables to serve as mixing stations. Make sure the mixing stations are away from the ingredients table and near electrical outlets. Set out a CD player to play soft sitar and other Indian music. Spread out colorful Indian print sheets or fabric on the floor in the center of the room.

MAKE IT HAPPEN   Dim the lights and allow for at least one hour of demonstration and instruction. Some instructors like to have soft music playing in the background. Ask your instructor ahead of time to ensure that you have music and audio equipment available, if desired. Some teens are very self-conscious of their bodies, so always ask before taking photos at the event. Then allow another thirty to forty-five minutes for smoothie preparation and consumption.

MARCH PASSIVE PROGRAMS

Fast Food Trivia. Make a list of ten popular meal choices at local fast-food restaurants, and ask teens to rank them from most healthy to most fattening and unhealthy. Most major chains list their products' fat content online or on packaging, or will provide this information upon request. Teens will be surprised to find the high fat content in tuna fish on thick tomato bread, for example.

March Music Mania. If there is a music listening station in the library, consider a Name That Tune type of contest. Use a Now CD or another mix with a variety of popular hits and have teens list the artist or title for the first three or four songs. Amy has a jukebox-style listening station and she put in ten popular CD albums that could not be seen. Teens were given a numbered form and asked to name as many album titles or artists as they could. A listening station with a shuffle could be loaded with a few albums or songs and teens could be asked to name three or four songs or artists. Or try One-Hit Wonders: Have teens match the name of a top-ten single to the name of an artist who made the top ten only once.

MARCH RESOURCES   There are many titles on different eras, but these are a few that highlight fashions and women's issues from various time periods.

Women in History   Epstein, Dan. *Twentieth-Century Pop Culture: The 70's*. Philadelphia: Chelsea House, 2001.

Leisch, Juanita. *Who Wore What? Women's Wear 1861–1965*. Gettysburg, PA: Thomas, 1995.

Pendergast, Sara, and Tom Pendergast. *Bowling, Beatniks, and Bell-Bottoms*. 5 vols. Detroit: UXL, 2002.

Schenone, Laura. *A Thousand Years over a Hot Stove*. New York: Norton, 2003.

> ### *Display Ideas*
> Dolls dressed as famous women from history, inventions by women. Or, set up a display if possible of some of the accessories or costumes to be used in the program in the library prior to the event, to stir interest. Large photos could also be used, but the actual items (in a case) will work best.

Friendship Bracelets   Torres, Laura. *Friendship Bracelets*. Palo Alto, CA: Klutz, 1996.

Smoothie Recipes   Barber, Mary Corpening. *Smoothies: Fifty Recipes for High-Energy Refreshment*. New York: Chronicle, 1999.

Beck, Sally Ann. *Smoothies, Sparklers, Shakes, and Coolers*. New York: Black Dog and Leventhal, 2002.

> ***Display Ideas***
> Blenders, old-fashioned glasses with straws, plastic fruits

Gabriel, Constans. *Great American Smoothies: The Ultimate Blending Guide for Shakes, Slushes, Desserts, and Thirst Quenchers*. New York: Avery, 1997.

Hirsch, Anita. *Drink to Your Health: Delicious Easy-to-Prepare Juices, Smoothies, Teas, Soups, and Other Beverages That Deliver Vitality and Immunity*. New York: Marlowe, 2000.

McIntyre, Anne. *Drink to Your Health*. New York: Simon and Schuster, 2000.

Roditzky, Donna Pliner. *Summer Smoothies: Over 130 Cool and Refreshing Recipes*. Roseville, CA: Prima, 2002.

———. *Ultimate Smoothies: Delicious Recipes for Over 125 of the Best Smoothies, Freezes, and Blasts*. Roseville, CA: Prima, 2000.

Titus, Dan. *Smoothies! The Original Smoothie Book: Recipes from the Pros*. Chino Hills, CA: Juice Gallery, 2000.

April

April sees teens develop even stronger spring fever and emotions as they prepare for the end of the year with all its changes and events. With National Poetry Month and National Library Week, there are many opportunities for programs highlighting creative teens. National Library Week also provides a chance to begin building momentum for summer reading events and to develop a mailing list for those events. Some other ideas include an Experience the Renaissance program or starting a knitting club.

Poetry Contest

Many teens like to read and write poetry. Writing poetry is a simple yet powerful way for teens to express emotions and for librarians to introduce teens to creative writing. April is National Poetry Month, the perfect time to encourage poetry writing by having a contest. Current and new writers will be attracted to this opportunity to showcase their work and to win prizes.

PREPARATION TIME	3 hours
LENGTH OF PROGRAM	1 month
NUMBER OF TEENS	No more than 50 (1 poem per teen)
SUGGESTED AGE RANGE	12–18 years; it is possible to split the competition into two divisions—one for junior high and one for senior high

SHOPPING LIST Prizes for winners, possibly to be purchased after seeing how many students enter

Small tokens of appreciation for judges and for teachers of participants

Optional incentive prize, such as an autographed book or a journal, for the teacher or class with the most entries

SETUP Most of the effort involved in this program will be spent on planning and marketing. By having the program in April, you will be competing with spring break and religious holidays during most years. You will have to decide if you want to publicize the winners during April, which would be especially appropriate during National Library Week, or after the month is over. It is always nice to have a program like this in conjunction with an author visit. The author does not have to be famous; local authors work very well. Winners of the poetry contest could have a meal with or get a specially autographed book from the author as part of the program.

No matter when the winners will be publicized, be certain to allow three to four weeks for submissions. If the submission period is any shorter, teachers may not have time to work the contest into their plans, and if the submission period is any longer, the contest will lose momentum and teens will forget about it. Mid-March through the first week in April is a workable timeline and could allow two weeks for judging before winners are announced.

It is crucial to get teachers on board. Also, develop any rules needed for the contest and select judges. Rules may specify language allowed, if that is important at your library. Because it is crucial not to stifle creativity, the topic of appropriate language can be treated lightly. Suggesting a theme, feature, or format, such as fantasy, rhyming, or sonnets, can be fun and inspiring, but freestyle should also be allowed.

One Month before Entries Are Submitted Get announcements about the poetry contest into all library brochures. Send notices to all teachers who have contacted you or participated in programs through the library in the past. Note that either students may e-mail their entries directly to you or the teacher may submit a class's entries in a group. If you have had low participation in the past, you may want to offer some incentive, such as journals or poetry books, to the teacher whose students submit the most entries. Be sure to get publicity out well before spring break. While you will want to mention when winners will be announced, do not state how many winners will be chosen or identify specific prizes. It is best to say something on the order of "Winners will be given gift certificates to area bookstores or autographed books, among other prizes."

Choose judges. It is always best to have young adults among them—members of a teen advisory board work well. Other judges may include library staff, teachers, and community members who work well with teens. When judges represent a cross-section of the community, they will probably choose poems based on how enjoyable they are and not necessarily on literary merit, which should be ok. Young adults will perceive that the contest is fun, they will like the winners, and they will not be as intimidated as they would be if winning poems were expected to be literary masterpieces. You can list criteria for judging to help guide the process.

Let managers of local bookstores know about the event. They will likely offer to have a contest-related display or some kind of discount on poetry books. They may be willing to let the winners read their work at an in-store event when the contest is over. If they do not, you may want to showcase the winners yourself at a coffeehouse night. Just remember that not all writers want to be performers. Issue an open invitation to anyone who entered the contest and offer some other kind of entertainment, either musical or dramatic, to help keep the pressure down.

Counseling centers are a great source of creative teens. The staff may well know which teens are looking to express themselves and are likely to pass along information about the contest to the young people in their care.

Two Weeks before Entries Are Submitted
Set up a display of poetry materials for young adults. Be sure to present a diverse selection, including rap, limericks, and bilingual poems. If any portion of the contest is theme-based, feature examples of that as well. Make bookmarks instead of traditional flyers describing the program and tuck them into the books in the display, new young adult books, and any other fast-moving items. Mail or e-mail reminders about the program to those who have participated in the past or who attend library events regularly.

MAKE IT HAPPEN
When e-mail entries are submitted, make certain that you can open them properly. E-mail the senders back right away, thanking them for their entries. Begin preliminary judging as the poems come in and develop a finalist pile. Make copies for each of the judges, being careful to omit the names on all copies but your master set. Ask each judge to rank his or her top three poems if there are fewer than twenty-five entries, or the top five poems if there are more than twenty-five entries. Or, if only a prize or two are available and there are many excellent entries, select some poems for honorable mention. Assign points to the poems based on the judges' rankings and average the totals for each poem. Having scores from many judges helps soften any complaints that may arise from the selection of the winners.

Announce winners in several ways, including posting the names and poems on the library website and on bulletin boards in the library. After contacting the winners, it is a good idea to send letters to their school principals so that the principals can publicize the students' success. Also mention any teachers who submitted many entries in support of the contest. Teachers who submitted entries from an entire class as well as judges should also receive a letter or a small thank-you gift from you, such as a bookmark or a token Starbucks gift certificate. This will help motivate them to participate in the contest again.

Send letters out as soon as possible to students who did not win, even if their teachers submitted their entries as part of a group. (See the sample nonwinners' letter in the appendix.) Include information about other places they could get published, and encourage them to enter future contests. Young adults can be discouraged so easily that this letter must be very positive. Enter the contact information from all participants, including teachers, into a database that can be used to print labels or postcards the next time you have a contest.

If only a handful of students enter the contest, perhaps all entries could be published through the library, with the winners in front. It may take a few contests to build up attention. One advantage: a small number of entries is easier to judge than hundreds of entries!

This may be a good opportunity to develop a creative writing journal through the library to maintain the momentum of the contest throughout the summer. Invite writers to send material and at least for the first few issues publish all of it, either on a website or in print. Be certain to have a copy catalogued for the library collection for posterity.

Experience the Renaissance

Contributed by Carol Marlowe, Rahway Public Library, Rahway, New Jersey

This program is a series of three two-hour art workshops focusing on the use of different methods and materials. The first session is on painting with watercolors, the second session is on sculpting with clay, and the final session is on mixed media. The program is intended to be presented by hired experts, but a variation is offered that can be presented by library staff.

PREPARATION TIME
2 hours, including contacting instructors and planning sessions, plus 1 hour of setup for each session

LENGTH OF PROGRAM
three 2-hour sessions

NUMBER OF TEENS
20

SUGGESTED AGE RANGE
12–18 years

SHOPPING LIST
If you plan to hire experts, ask them what supplies need to be purchased for their workshops. If staff will present the workshops, it may be a good idea to seek advice at an arts supply or crafts store about the best beginner materials for working with clay, paints, and glues and paper for collage.

SETUP

Two Months before Program

The three sessions based on this model each focused on a different type of art: the first on painting with watercolors, the second on sculpting with clay, and the third on mixed media. When hiring experts, ask for a demonstration with time allowed for hands-on creativity. It is important to go over the following setup questions with session leaders:

> What specific supplies will be needed for each participant in each session?
>
> Will the expert bring the necessary supplies, or will staff need to purchase them?
>
> How should the room be set up?
>
> Will audiovisual equipment be needed?
>
> Are there specific electrical needs?
>
> Will maintenance staff be needed to help carry supplies?
>
> Will teens be leaving their projects to dry or harden between sessions? If so, what kind of area will be needed?

One Month before Program

Make sure the schools know about this series, as it could tie in to history as well as art studies. Arts-and-crafts stores are another venue in which to advertise the program. Advertising should clearly state the nature of the artwork, if any, that teens will be bringing home and specify whether the work will be finished or require further effort. This program lends itself to creative displays, with the possibility of colorful backgrounds, prints of paintings from the Renaissance, and the like.

MAKE IT HAPPEN

The Rahway Public Library hired the Phoenix Arts Group to help teens appreciate the different forms of art and to enhance the teens' confidence in their abilities. This program could be adapted by hiring different experts for the different media or by asking senior high art students to demonstrate for the younger set. Art teachers also may be willing to run the workshop.

Variation

If you are going to run the program yourself or with volunteers, it can be offered as one two-hour workshop or as two two-hour workshops. Interest in the different art media may expand this effort into a teen art club. Have materials for different types of art set up at different stations where a few teens could work on a project, then move on to another while the first one dries. For example, one table could hold clay and sculpting tools. The next table could have drawing materials and books with examples of how to draw animals, people, or some other subject. A third table or another session could explore two types of painting. It is important in this variation to answer the setup questions presented under "Two Months before Program," only with staff instead of experts. The supplies and room setup needs will also be considerations.

To fill time when people are waiting for projects to dry or be completed, have a Cranium board game available. It utilizes many skills, including molding with clay and drawing.

Knitting Club

Knitting has become very popular and chic in the last few years, with famous stars such as Julia Roberts and Sandra Bullock taking up needles. Long scarves have become fashionable. Teaching teens a craft can give them a way to express themselves creatively for the rest of their lives. Knitting is something they can enjoy in a group or work on by themselves while watching TV. It also is a way for them to volunteer to help others. This program is adapted from a very successful weekly one developed by the Mokena (IL) Public Library.

PREPARATION TIME   4 hours, including research and shopping

LENGTH OF PROGRAM   1-day teaching session: 3 hours

NUMBER OF TEENS   5 teens per instructor or helper

SUGGESTED AGE RANGE   Grades 5–12 (If interest is high and many teens catch on to knitting, invite them to teach children in grades 4–6 at another session.)

SHOPPING LIST   Several skeins of worsted-weight yarn in teen-appealing colors to make blanket squares or hats

Several sets of needles to match the yarn, probably sizes 7–8

Skeins of fun fur eyelash yarn for girls' scarves and bulky wool for boys' scarves

Several pairs of size 11 needles for scarves

Large Ziploc bags for projects

SETUP   This program lends itself to several different formats. Great popularity may lead to regular club meetings.

Hire a local knitter to come and teach teens how to knit. Or ask library staff who knit to come and work with the teens. There should be no more than five beginners for each knitter. Take registration for this program, and charge a small fee to ensure that registered teens will come and to help offset the cost of materials, which participants should be able to take home with them. Possible formats include

Three to four sessions, three hours each. In this format, teens should be able to finish a project such as a scarf or hat.

Weekly or Monthly Knit Café or Club, two- to three-hour sessions. In this format, teens can be introduced to new techniques or projects at the beginning of each session, with treats and time for working. Teens can also make and collect squares for blankets to donate to charity. This is an enjoyable after-school drop-in project.

One Month before Program It may be a good idea to survey teens and older grade school children ahead of time to get an idea of the possible interest for this event, as it will require an investment of research time and materials. However, only a few interested young people are needed to get this off the ground. As more people see them and what they are working on, interest will build.

Research local craft and discount stores for cost of materials. Some stores may even donate yarn and needles. Ask whether store personnel would be willing to teach knitting to teens.

If you are not a knitter, using local expert help is a good idea, or poll staff to see who is willing and able to help you. Library staff are amazingly creative people and it is likely that someone at your facility can be of service. Be sure to familiarize yourself with the basics so that you are comfortable using the knitting and purling stitches. Teens may not mind if you learn with them, but there should be someone available to help with problems. Watch videos and look at books to help yourself as well.

MAKE IT HAPPEN Set out enough yarns to give teens some choice in what they want to make. If they are going to spend lots of time and possible frustration on a project, they should at least like the results. When teens walk in, they should see attractive materials on display, with beginners' books on knitting for those who want to continue to study the craft after the class. It may be a good idea to have a take-home list of further resources, including how-to books, places to buy materials, and knitting websites for teens. To further inspire the participants, bring in expensive knitted garments and some that have been hand knitted and see if they can tell the difference.

Depending on the format, there should be some instructional time and some independent working time. While it would be hard to have refreshments at a program where hands need to be clean, it is possible to have music playing while teens are working. Comfortable chairs and plenty of light should also be provided. Arranging the chairs around tables provides space for balls of yarn and printed instructions.

Variations *Intergenerational Knitting.* Bring your teen advisory board to a local senior center to knit with them, or to have the two age groups teach each other how to knit. You could also have an intergenerational knitting program at the library by advertising that at least two generations of family members should attend together.

Knitting for Charity. Hats, scarves, and blankets are always needed by someone. Just like the Origami Patriotic Peace Project described in the November chapter, this could be a good program to demonstrate at different agencies who serve teens in your area. Or, if no one on the library staff can knit and demonstrate, perhaps someone from one of the other agencies would be willing to do workshops at both places to gather knitted items for charities. Beginners can also knit squares to be combined into a blanket for

Warm Up America. (See "Knitting for Charity" in this chapter's list of resources.)

Outreach to Detention Centers. Take adult staff volunteers to teach incarcerated teens in your area how to knit. Facilities may have rules about the types of needles that can be used, but there are many projects that call for very large knitting needles. The materials may also be collected at the end of the class. Incarcerated teens may get a great deal of satisfaction out of making things for others.

APRIL PASSIVE PROGRAMS

Quick Library Quiz. Create a sheet of questions about basic library facts, such as how long a CD-ROM may be checked out and the amounts of various fines. All the answers may be taken from a brochure about the library, or you could plan to display the answers on a poster after the quiz period is over. To encourage teens to participate, consider offering a small prize or piece of candy for turning in a finished quiz. Or quizzes with all questions answered correctly could be entered in a raffle for a gift certificate or book.

Librarian Legends. This is a different way of having fun with library trivia. Make up some wild librarian stories interspersed with true ones, and ask teens to indicate which tales are true and which are false. Make up a poster with the answers and enliven it with pictures of stereotypical librarians or of current library staff. Either offer an incentive prize for participating or draw a name for a larger prize, as with the Quick Library Quiz, or use both strategies.

National Poetry Month. Offer a rhyming couplet contest or a contest for the best poem that uses library words. (Provide a short list of familiar terms.) Post entries without names on a bulletin board or on a simple handout and have teens or staff vote on favorites. Offer little prizes for entering and award larger prizes, such as journals or books of poetry, to winners.

APRIL RESOURCES

Poetry

Display Ideas

A magnetic poetry kit with a metal board, or for a larger version, a sizable felt board with cutout words that are laminated and backed with Velcro; quill pens, journals, thesauruses

Cart, Michael, ed. *Rush Hour: Sin . . .* New York: Delacorte, 2004.

Clinton, Catherine, ed. *A Poem of Her Own: Voices of American Women Yesterday and Today.* New York: Abrams, 2003.

Corrigan, Eireann. *You Remind Me of You: A Poetry Memoir.* New York: Scholastic, 2002.

Fields, Terri. *After the Death of Anna Gonzales.* New York: Henry Holt, 2002.

Grimes, Nikki. *Bronx Masquerade.* New York: Dial, 2002.

High, Linda Oatman. *Sister Slam and the Poetic Motormouth Roadtrip.* New York: Bloomsbury Children's Books, 2004.

Major, Devorah. *Where River Meets Ocean.* San Francisco: City Lights Foundation, 2003.

Meyer, John, and Stephanie Meyer, eds. *Teen Ink: Written in the Dirt.* Deerfield Beach, FL: Health Communications, 2004.

Paint Me Like I Am: Teen Poems from WritersCorps. New York: HarperTempest, 2003.

Rosenberg, Liz. *Seventeen: A Novel in Prose Poems.* Chicago: Cricket, 2002.

Tom, Karen, Matt Frost, and Kiki. *Angst! Teen Verses from the Edge.* New York: Workman, 2001.

Renaissance Teens

The Renaissance

Barter, James. *A Renaissance Painter's Studio.* San Diego: Lucent, 2003.

Cohen, Elizabeth Storr. *Daily Life in Renaissance Italy.* Westport, CN: Greenwood, 2001.

Goffen, Rona. *Renaissance Rivals: Michelangelo, Leonardo, Raphael, Titian.* New Haven, CN: Yale University Press, 2002.

Hartt, Frederick. *History of Italian Renaissance Art: Painting, Sculpture, Architecture.* New York: Abrams, 2003.

> ### Display Ideas
> Pieces from the Cranium game to play with, including the clay; or paintbrushes, office desk create-a-sculptures, magnetic David and clothes on a metal board

Art Forms

Albus, Anita. *The Art of Arts: Rediscovering Painting.* New York: Knopf, 2000.

Dewey, Katherine. *Creating Lifelike Animals in Polymer Clay.* Maxwell, TX: Elvenwork, 2000.

Kallenberg, Lawrence. *Modeling in Wax for Jewelry and Sculpture.* 2nd ed. Iola, WI: Krause, 2000.

Moran, Patricia. *The Oil Painter's Ultimate Flower and Portrait Companion.* Verde, NV: International Artist, 2000.

Nelson, Craig. *Sixty Minutes to Better Painting.* Cincinnati: North Light, 2002.

Plowman, John. *The Encyclopedia of Sculpting Techniques.* Philadelphia: Running Press, 1995.

Price, Morgan Samuel. *Oil Painting with a Basic Palette.* Cincinnati: North Light, 1999.

Saper, Chris. *Painting Beautiful Skin Tones with Color and Light.* Cincinnati: North Light, 2001.

Knitting

Carles, Julie, and Jordana Jacobs. *The Yarn Girls Guide to Simple Knits.* New York: Clarkson Potter, 2002.

Mellor, Zoe. *Easy Knits: Learn to Knit the Easy Way through Ten Simple Projects.* Cincinnati: North Light, 2003.

Display Ideas
Needles and yarn balls, attractive knitted scarves or other knitted objects

Melville, Sally. *The Knitting Experience: Book 1; Knit Stitch*. Sioux Falls, SD: XRX, 2002.

———. *The Knitting Experience: Book 2; Purl Stitch*. Sioux Falls, SD: XRX, 2003.

Wenger, Jennifer, et al. *Teen Knitting Club: Chill Out and Knit*. New York: Artisan, 2004.

Zimmerman, Elizabeth. *Knitting without Tears*. New York: Scribner, 1971.

Knitting for Charity

Caps for Kids: http://www.capsforkids.org. This organization collects hats and more for children in need.

Project Linus: http://www.projectlinus.org. Sewn, knitted, or crocheted blankets are collected for children in hospitals or otherwise in dire need.

Warm Up America: http://www.warmupamerica.com. This group collects both blankets and seven-by-nine-inch squares to be made into blankets for people in need.

May

May is a busy time for teens as they go through end-of-school-year rituals. Some fun and appropriate programs during this time include a Mother-Daughter Book Discussion, Cake Decorating, and a Photography Contest. The cake-decorating and photography skills come in especially handy at this time of year for teens, with the many graduation ceremonies and rituals. These programs can help set a festive mood at the library before you head into the summer reading events.

Mother-Daughter Book Discussion

Invite female teens to celebrate Mother's Day with a book discussion for them and their mothers. The event will include ice-breaking games and fun activities but may ultimately help open channels of communication.

PREPARATION TIME	4 hours, including time to choose a book, prepare discussion questions, plan an ice-breaker activity, and set up the room
LENGTH OF PROGRAM	2 hours
NUMBER OF TEENS	15 plus their (or someone else's) mothers
SUGGESTED AGE RANGE	Grades 5–10

SHOPPING LIST	15 copies of the chosen book
	Food: pink lemonade or iced tea, cookies or finger sandwiches, small fruits or cut-up fruit
	Pink paper tablecloths
	Spring flowers for centerpieces

SETUP

One Month before Program

Find a book that deals with the mother-daughter relationship. Good relationships are nice, but bad ones make for much livelier discussions. When mother-daughter teams sign up for the program, they should receive a copy of the book along with a few questions to think about. Some sample books and questions are presented below. Complete book information is included in the resource list for May.

The Usual Rules, by Joyce Maynard

- What are some of the different ways in which Wendy and the other characters in the book handle tragedy?
- How do think you would react in a similar situation?
- If you could go anywhere you wanted and start fresh, where would you go?
- What is the biggest lesson Wendy learns from her friends in California?

I Love You Mom! by Kelly Ripa and Diane Clehane

- How has your mom made an impact on your life?
- What kind of mom (or influence) do you think you will be?

A Mother's Gift, by Britney and Lynne Spears

- What kind of relationship did Holly and her mother, Wanda, have? How does your relationship with your mother compare?
- Would you give up everything, including your family, to follow your dreams?
- Does success really change people? How did success at her new school change Holly?

One Hour before Program

Think pink! And flowery. Set up tables with four chairs apiece, enough for two mothers and two daughters. Cover the tables with pink paper tablecloths and use spring bouquets for centerpieces. Supply enough pens or pencils and writing paper for four people.

Set up the refreshment table. Pink lemonade would work really well for this event. Also give the option of tea and coffee to drink. Arrange trays with cookies or finger sandwiches and fresh fruit.

MAKE IT HAPPEN

Ice Breakers

Once all the mothers and daughters have arrived, start by having some sort of ice breaker. Try having participants list five of their favorite things when they were five years old and explain why those things were so important to them. Or play How Well Do You Know Your Mother/Daughter? Give each mother-daughter pair six to ten questions to answer about each other, such as "What time does your mother usually get up?" "What is your daughter's favorite TV show?" "What is your mother's favorite outfit?" "What does your daughter like to do after school?" Read the questions and have each pair answer them on paper. Then read the answers aloud to see which mother-daughter team knows each other best.

Book Discussion

Open the book discussion with the questions that were distributed with the book. Also ask some general questions, such as

> What was your favorite part of the story?
>
> Who was your favorite character?
>
> Why did [name of character] do _____?
>
> What do you think the author meant by the phrase "_____"? Ask both daughters and mothers to think about what they liked about the child and the parent in the book and what they disliked. How do their responses relate to their own relationship?

Make sure that all participants get to ask any questions that they have and that those questions are discussed. For best results, let the girls answer each question first so that the mothers do not take over the discussion.

Mother-Daughter Poetry

Have each daughter write the first line of a poem and give the paper to her mother when she is done. Each mother writes the next line and gives the paper back to her daughter. Ask each pair to continue passing their poem back and forth until they have written six to ten lines. At the end of the activity, ask each pair to read their poem out loud to the group. You may suggest a theme for the poems or help the group pick a theme together.

Cake Decorating

Contributed by Carol Marlowe,
Rahway Public Library, Rahway,
New Jersey

There are lots of parties at the end of the school year to celebrate religious ceremonies, graduations, concerts, and the like. Teach teens how to do their own cake decorating, either by demonstrating techniques from books or by hiring a professional to run the program. One of the best parts of this program is that samples can be eaten!

PREPARATION TIME

4 hours, including baking cupcakes, shopping, and setting up the room; to save time, three unfrosted cupcakes per participant may be purchased rather than home baked

LENGTH OF PROGRAM

3 hours

NUMBER OF TEENS

10–25

SUGGESTED AGE RANGE

12 years and up

SHOPPING LIST

Cake-decorating kits

Cupcake liners

Cake mixes (plan on three cupcakes per participant)

Frostings

Decorating gels

SETUP

One Week before Program

If library staff will run the program, purchase a cake-decorating kit or frosting gels with different tips and practice making simple leaves, flowers, and border decorations by following instructions in cake-decorating books.

One Day before Program

Bake at least three cupcakes per registered teen plus extras for demonstration. Use a mix and paper liners so that teens can replicate the cupcakes at home. Some libraries and schools have policies stating that food must be purchased from commercial sources instead of prepared in homes. If this is the case at your library, make advance arrangements with a local bakery or grocery store to supply plain, unfrosted cupcakes for the program.

Day of Program

Have samples of different types of decorative writing available for teens to look at. Choose simple types that could easily be done in frosting. It is also a good idea to pull library books on cake decorating so that teens can see pictures of different styles and themes.

MAKE IT HAPPEN

Set up the room with one table or counter where staff can demonstrate while teens watch plus a number of smaller tables where teens can work on their own cupcakes.

Demonstrate how to use the different tools in a cake-decorating kit, including how to make flowers. Have teens think about their designs before they attempt them with the frosting. Allow time for them to peruse the idea books and to sketch their designs. Suggest that they keep their first attempt fairly simple, but specify that you do want each teen to learn a new technique or two, such as flower making.

Invite the teens to work on their own projects. Be sure to have enough cupcakes that each participant can decorate two or three. Take photos.

Variation   It is possible to invite a professional to run this program, such as someone from a vocational school or bakery. A staff member who has taken a decorating class may also be willing to demonstrate basic skills.

Photography Contest

May is an important time for teens. The end of the school year is coming, with graduations, honor ceremonies, friends departing, and important social occasions. To encourage budding photographers to capture those events, create a contest. Invite teens to bring in their photographs for judging and a ceremony. You can purchase disposable cameras ahead of time for teens who do not have a camera.

PREPARATION TIME   5 hours

LENGTH OF PROGRAM   1–2 hours for awards ceremony

NUMBER OF TEENS   25

SUGGESTED AGE RANGE   Grades 7–12

SHOPPING LIST   Disposable cameras
Food: cookies, lemonade or iced tea
Ribbons for winners
Prizes such as gift certificates to a camera store

SETUP

One Month before Program   Ask around town, the university, galleries, photo shops, news organizations, and the like to find an expert willing to judge the contest. Also try to find someone (perhaps the same person) to give a photography talk, with information on how to get started, basic techniques, and how to choose a camera.

Two Hours before Program   Construction paper cameras are not too hard to make. Cut out a black rectangle, and paste in the middle of it a white circle, with a smaller black circle in the middle for the shutter. Cut out a smaller black rectangle and glue this to the upper right side to resemble a flash. Make a number of cameras and attach them to the walls and tabletops. Also, if you can find old reels of discarded film, hang them around the room as you would with rolls of crepe paper.

One Hour before Program   Tack the photos brought in for judging around the walls of the room. Have the judge put ribbons under the best-in-show pieces.

MAKE IT HAPPEN   Offer refreshments to teens as they come in for the ceremony and program. Anything will work for this: lemonade, punch, soda, and so forth.

To add to the atmosphere of this event, think of something to hand out related to photography. For example, save old film canisters and fill them with M&Ms to give to all the participants in the contest.

MAY PASSIVE PROGRAMS

For both programs below, display the photos to be identified on a poster. After the quiz period is over, write the answers under the photos right on the poster, or type the answers using a word-processing program and cut and glue the text onto the poster. Offer small prizes for teens who have no more than one incorrect guess.

Photo Mystery. Put up numbered photos, taken from weird angles, of buildings in the area or places in the library. Make forms with corresponding numbered lines where teens can write their guesses of what each photo shows.

Famous Photos. Have numbered photos of ten famous city skylines or of the Seven Wonders of the World on a poster. Make forms with corresponding numbered lines where teens can write their guesses of what each photo shows.

MAY RESOURCES

Mothers and Daughters

Display Idea
Flowers

Cohen-Sandler, Roni. *Trust Me, Mom—Everyone Else Is Going! The New Rules for Mothering Adolescent Daughters*. New York: Penguin, 2003.

Forsyth, Sondra. *Girls Seen and Heard: Fifty-two Life Lessons for Our Daughters*. New York: Tarcher/Putnam, 1998.

Lara, Adair. *Hold Me Close, Let Me Go: A Mother, a Daughter, and Adolescence Survived*. New York: Broadway Books, 2001.

Maynard, Joyce. *The Usual Rules*. New York: St. Martin's, 2003.

McBride, Regina. *The Land of Women*. New York: Simon and Schuster, 2003.

Moriarty, Laura. *The Center of Everything*. New York: Hyperion, 2003.

Orgel, Doris. *My Mother's Daughter: Four Greek Goddesses Speak*. Brookfield, CT: Roaring Brook, 2003.

Pierson, Stephanie, and Phyllis Cohen. *You Have to Say I'm Pretty, You're My Mother: How to Help Your Daughter Learn to Love Her Body and Herself*. New York: Simon and Schuster, 2003.

Ripa, Kelly, and Diane Clehane, eds. *I Love You Mom! A Celebration of Our Mothers and Their Gifts to Us*. New York: Hyperion, 2003.

Shange, Ntozake. *Daddy Says*. New York: Simon and Schuster Books for Young Readers, 2003.

Shimko, Bonnie. *Letters in the Attic*. Chicago: Academy Chicago, 2002.

Spears, Britney, and Lynne Spears. *A Mother's Gift*. New York: Delacorte, 2001.

Stone, Miriam R. *At the End of Words: A Daughter's Memoirs*. Cambridge, MA: Candlewick, 2003.

Cake Decoration

Beginner's Guide to Cake Decorating. London: Merehurst, 2002.

Cook, Deanna. *FamilyFun Birthday Cakes*. New York: Disney, 2003.

Deacon, Carol. *The Complete Step-by-Step Guide to Cake Decorating*. Chanhassen, MN: Creative Publishers International, 2003.

———. *Two-Hour Party Cakes*. London: New Holland, 1999.

Fabulous Cake Decorating. Cincinnati: Betterway, 2000.

Healy, Bruce. *The Art of the Cake*. New York: Morrow, 1999.

Latour, Shalini. *The Icing on the Cake*. Cincinnati: North Light, 2004.

Maxfield, Jaynie. *Cake Decorating for the First Time*. New York: Sterling, 2003.

Miller, Marcianne. *The Artful Cupcake*. New York: Lark, 2004

Weinstock, Sylvia. *Sweet Celebrations*. New York: Simon and Schuster, 1999.

> ### *Display Ideas*
> Decorating implements such as cookie presses, pastry bags, nozzles for different shapes; place books for display on cake plates

Photography

Ang, Tom. *Digital Photography: An Introduction*. New York: DK, 2003.

Antrobus, Roger. *Selling Photography*. New York: Amphoto, 2003.

Enfield, Jill. *Photo-Imaging: A Complete Guide to Alternative Processes*. New York: Amphoto, 2003.

Freeman, Michael. *The Complete Guide to Digital Photography*. New York: Lark, 2004.

Friedman, Debra. *Picture This: Fun Photography and Crafts*. Toronto: Kids Can Press, 2003.

Gaines, Ann. *American Photographers: Capturing the Image*. Berkeley Heights, NJ: Enslow, 2002.

Glick, Susan. *One Shot*. New York: H. Holt, 2003.

Hoye, Jacob, and Walter Einenkel. *Diary*. New York: MTV Books/Pocket Books, 2003.

MTV. *MTV Photobooth*. New York: Universe, 2002.

Nathan, M. M. *MTV Cribs*. New York: Pocket Books, 2002.

The Polar Bear Waltz and Other Moments of Epic Silliness: Classic Photographs from Outside Magazine's "Parting Shot." New York: Norton, 2003.

Pring, Roger, and Ivan Hissey. *Make Your Own Digital Photo Scrapbook*. Lewes, East Sussex: Sterling, 2002.

Schaub, George. *Using Your Digital Camera*. New York: Amphoto, 2003.

Schulke, Flip, with Matt Schudel. *Witness to Our Times: My Life as a Photojournalist*. Chicago: Cricket, 2003.

Through the Lens: National Geographic Greatest Photographs. Washington, DC: National Geographic, 2003.

June

Summer at the library means summer reading, and lots of teens hanging around—we hope! While this book does not go into summer reading programs in detail, the appendix includes book logs from STDL and the Lawrence Public Library. The STDL program, Slay a Book, uses a combination of reading suggestions and programs in a bingo format while the Lawrence example for winter reading, Warm Up with a Good Book, uses a traditional book log. Different formats work in different settings.

Programming in the summer can be more elaborate than during the school year and can even span more than one session. Special events can also be held, such as a tie-dyeing workshop, an outdoor scavenger hunt, and a lock-in.

Tie-Dyeing for Teens

T-shirts and summer go hand in hand, and interest in tie-dyeing never wanes. In addition, tie-dyeing appeals to both boys and girls, making it a great summer program. Modern craft supplies can make tie-dyeing easier (see our beginner version or purchase a kit), or the traditional method can still be done. A fun tie-dyed cupcakes activity has also been included.

PREPARATION TIME 3–4 hours for shopping and setup of the cloth tie-dyeing versions; up to 5 hours when tie-dyed cupcakes are added

LENGTH OF PROGRAM 2–2½ hours, depending on whether cupcakes will be baked during the program

NUMBER OF TEENS	10–15
SUGGESTED AGE RANGE	Grades 7–12
SHOPPING LIST **Tie-Dyeing Option 1: Beginners**	Prewashed 100 percent cotton T-shirts or fabric to make socks, head-bands, a pillowcase, or a towel. *No polyester or blends.* If you have teens bring their own items to dye, make sure they prewash them before coming to the program.
	Permanent markers in assorted colors, ordinary fat-tipped ones as well as highlighters; rubbing alcohol; squeeze bottles; plastic gloves (no latex); rubber bands; disposable cups; large pieces of cardboard or white tag board (at least one piece for each person).
	Squeeze bottles and enough rubbing alcohol to fill them
	You will also need tables to work on and plastic and newspapers to cover the tables.
Tie-Dyeing Option 2: Advanced	Water—to soak, rinse, and make dye solution
	Prewashed 100 percent cotton T-shirts or fabric to make socks, head-bands, a pillowcase, or a towel. *No polyester or blends.* If you have teens bring their own items to dye, make sure they prewash them before coming to the program.
	Plastic gloves—at least 2 pairs for each person to protect hands
	At least 4–8 5-gallon buckets—to hold fixer solution and fabric for presoak
	1 big stick or spoon—to stir the solution in the 5-gallon bucket
	String or rubber bands—for binding the areas of fabric you want to keep white
	Powder dyes—the best dye to use on cotton is a good fiber reactive dye, such as Procion MX Fiber Reactive Dye. Such dyes are available at fabric and yarn stores or by mail order (try Dharma Trading Company at http://www.dharmatrading.com). Purchase anywhere from one color for a simple, single-color project to ten colors for advanced, multicolor designs. The number of colors will depend on your budget and the number of kids registered. Plan on one squeeze bottle or bucket for each color. Do not use RIT dyes for this project. They will not last as long, and they do not dissolve very well.
	Plastic sheets or bags and newspaper—to cover and protect the tables and floor if this program must take place indoors
	Fixer (soda ash)—to prepare the fabric for dyeing; or PH Plus, which may be purchased from a pool supply store
	Urea—a synthetic nitrogen compound used as a humectant in printing and painting with all classes of dyes. Urea has two purposes: it can make dyes dissolve more easily and it makes colors much stronger and brighter. Five pounds will do about 80 shirts.

Squeeze and spray bottles or eye droppers—to apply the dye in a variety of designs

Plastic garbage bags—to store the shirts in after you are done dyeing so teens can take them home

Scissors—to remove the string or rubber bands used to tie the shirts, if all steps are to be completed at the library

Large trash can—to dispose of messy newspapers during the program

Measuring cups and spoons

Photocopies of rinsing instructions, one for each participant

4–8 long tables to work on

SETUP

Day of Program

Set up several tables with chairs, allowing room for four to six people per table. Cover each table with newspaper and plastic. Fill the squeeze bottles with rubbing alcohol, and place all necessary supplies on the tables.

Tie-Dyeing Option 1:
Beginners

Fill the squeeze bottles with rubbing alcohol.

Place rubber bands, cups, and tag board or cardboard on tables.

Tie-Dyeing Option 2:
Advanced

This is an outside event. It is just not wise to do advanced tie-dyeing inside unless the library plans to start remodeling the very next day and a huge mess will not matter. The dyes you use are permanent. The water is wet. Outside!

The night before or the morning of the event mix the dye using the directions on the container because the amount required differs from color to color. And always, always cover your face with a mask or bandana so you will not breathe in the powdered dye.

You may use either buckets or bottles to apply the dye. If you are doing the program outside, consider using buckets to soak the garments. This way is much more fun, but it takes a lot of room. Squeeze bottles are sometimes easier and a little less messy. Both approaches use the same recipe for dye, but in one case you fill buckets with the dye and in the other you pour the dye into the plastic bottles. You will need as many bottles as you have colors of dye. If you want multiple bottles of each color, you will need additional bottles. Note that squeeze bottles are used only if buckets are not. In addition, eye droppers may be used to apply dye in small places or spaces. You fill the dropper bottles with dye and use the droppers to drip dye onto the shirts.

Outside, set up four different dyeing stations. Each one will consist of one or two long tables. Cover each table with plastic sheets or garbage bags. Cover the garbage bags with three layers of newspapers.

Fill two five-gallon buckets halfway with water (2½ gallons). In one bucket, add 2½ pounds of soda ash. The other bucket of water is for rinsing.

On each work table, put two or three bottles of dye (if you are using bottles) and a pile of string or rubber bands.

MAKE IT HAPPEN

Tie-Dyeing Option 1: Beginners

Demonstrate one or more of the techniques for tie-dyeing described below. Then invite teens to create their own tie-dye designs.

Stretch a section of shirt over the opening of a sturdy disposable cup and secure it with a rubber band. Draw a design in marker. Apply the alcohol and allow the color to bleed.

Place a piece of cardboard inside the shirt. Draw the desired design. Apply the alcohol and allow the color to bleed. This method allows a larger section of shirt to be decorated but also uses larger amounts of alcohol.

Draw a design on a section of shirt, gather the section and rubber band it tightly, and then dip the area in alcohol. Or, wear gloves and smear the marker with your hands as the alcohol is applied.

Tie-Dyeing Option 2: Advanced

As teens arrive send them to a station and have them presoak their items in the ash water for ten minutes. When everyone is ready, demonstrate to the entire group the different methods of folding or rolling the garments and tying them up with string or rubber bands.

To make a circle, pull up from the center of the fabric to create a handle. With a rubber band, start at the base of the fabric and twist the band around the handle over and over, until you reach the top. Make sure the rubber band is nice and tight.

For a straight-line pattern, fold the material into a fan or accordion shape. Then tie the fabric along the entire length of the fold with several rubber bands.

Let teens play with different patterns. Just remind them of two things: (1) wherever the rubber bands are is where they will get the pattern and (2) the bands must be kept tight so that the dye will not leak into a part of the pattern where it does not belong.

When teens have finished folding fabric and placing rubber bands, have them put the fabric into their dye of choice and let it sit for five or ten minutes. (Now is a good time for tie-dye cupcakes if you are going to have snacks. See instructions below.)

After the garments are dyed, but while they are still wet, have the teens put them in plastic garbage bags. To be on the safe side, put each bag inside yet another plastic garbage bag to prevent leakage and avoid upsetting parents.

Give each teen a photocopy of the rinsing instructions (see the appendix) and a clean pair of plastic gloves to take home. Before the teens leave, to make sure they understand the process, go over the instructions with them and allow them to ask questions.

Helpful Hints

Where teens place the rubber bands will determine where the colors go, so make sure they understand that.

Put down plastic sheets wherever you will be working. No matter which version of tie-dyeing you use, this program is messy!

EXTRA ACTIVITY: Tie-Dye Cupcakes

PREPARATION TIME	1 hour for shopping and setup
LENGTH OF PROGRAM	90 minutes
NUMBER OF TEENS	10–20
SUGGESTED AGE RANGE	11–18 years
SHOPPING LIST	For 12 teens:

> 1 box white or yellow cake mix
>
> $^2/_3$ cup multicolored sprinkles (we used Betty Crocker Parlor Perfect Confetti Sprinkles)
>
> Betty Crocker Easy Color Decorating Spray in blue, yellow, and red
>
> 24 baking cups
>
> 2½ cups white frosting

SETUP Cover the table and the floor around it with newspaper or plastic. Gather all required measuring cups, bowls, bakeware, and utensils. Preheat the oven according to the instructions on the cake mix box.

MAKE IT HAPPEN The description below assumes that teens will bake their own cupcakes. Some libraries may not have facilities to use for baking or may not allow items baked at home by staff to be eaten by teens. In such cases ask a bakery for plain baked cupcakes in paper liners, enough for at least two per teen.

1. Prepare the cake batter according to the directions on the box. Stir the sprinkles into the finished batter and fill the baking cups half full. Bake as directed for cupcakes.

2. Allow the cupcakes to cool completely.

3. Cover your work area and then, following the directions on the decorating spray bottle, spray blue circles on the cupcakes. Next, spray yellow rings around the blue circles. Finish decorating the cupcakes by covering the rest of the white frosting with the red decorating spray.

Makes 24 cupcakes.

Road Rally on Foot

Scavenger hunts in the library are fun, but consider taking it to a new level by moving it outside the building. Depending on where the library is located, this program can have different variations. The object is to have teens answer questions around the community, preferably by walking. For example, what does a statue in the center of town represent? What year is marked on the time capsule outside the library?

PREPARATION TIME	5 hours
LENGTH OF PROGRAM	2 hours
NUMBER OF TEENS	32 in teams of up to 4 members
SUGGESTED AGE RANGE	Grades 7–12
SHOPPING LIST	Prizes for the winning team at least—something small like novelties or paperback books
	Food for a post-hunt activity, such as an ice cream sundae bar with fixings
	Optional: Water guns for staff

SETUP

One Month before Program

Identify several places teens could walk to safely within a short distance of the library. Speak with the managers of any retail places where you would like teens to go to make sure they are willing to participate. Some may even be willing to give teens some token, such as a sticker or flyer or pencil, to prove they were there.

Do not plan on having teens go to more than six or seven stops, including any areas of the library where they might seek answers to questions.

One Week before Program

Prepare the questionnaires that will guide teens on their hunt. It may be a good idea to walk through the stops to make sure the answers are readily available. Make an answer key for staff as you do this.

Teams will finish the hunt at different rates, so plan some sort of activity or refreshments to occupy them when they return to the library. An ice cream sundae bar is easy to set up with bowls of fixings such as sprinkles, cherries, sliced bananas, strawberries, nuts, sauces, and whipped toppings.

If teens will need to visit retail shops, remind the managers when the teens will be stopping by.

Day of Program

Plan on having staff at various checkpoints to keep an eye on teens moving from place to place. It may be fun for staff to use water guns to spray (lightly, of course) teams who may not be following the rules. It is also a good idea to require teens to check in with staff at a halfway point.

Set up any markers needed at the locations. These can be construction-paper stars on trees near checkpoints.

One staff member can set up the snacks and wait in the meeting room for the teams to come in. Teens who register individually can be matched up into teams.

For preregistered teams, set up tables where they can read copies of the rules before starting the game.

MAKE IT HAPPEN   When the teens have arrived, run through the rules for the program:

> Teams must stick together. They cannot separate to save time finding answers.
>
> Teams must go in the order on their sheet. Have each team start on a different question and proceed in order, or print out different versions of the questionnaire, each starting with a different question. While teams will need to travel to the locations in the specified order, they should not all be in the same place at the same time. The retail places will thank you!
>
> Teens cannot run. Those that do may become targets for roving staff members with water guns.
>
> All teams must check in at a midway point.
>
> Teens must be respectful in retail outlets.
>
> Teens should have between one hour and ninety minutes to complete the road rally, depending on how many questions are provided. Be sure to specify a definite ending time, or you may have a team who lags way behind.

Note: When making the questionnaires, be sure to leave space at the top for the team name and finish time. Some teams may come in at the same time, and this information will give staff a way to document their arrival.

Sample Questions   (Include some in-house library questions if you prefer.)

> What is the most expensive price of pickles in [name of grocery store]?
>
> Who offers "the best coffee in town"? (Use a slogan in a window. Then teens will not need to go in.)
>
> What are three new releases at [name of video store]?
>
> What time does [name of park] close?

Variation: A Real Road Rally   Instead of limiting this program to locations within walking distance of the library, it is possible to extend it to locations throughout the community. Rather than staging it as a one-day event, which might lead some teens to drive too quickly, consider having it as a part of summer reading. It could be done as a one-week trivia game to encourage teens to get to know the community. Teens could have police sign their sheet, or town officials. Everyone who finishes would get a prize.

Lock-In

Everybody loves a sleepover and there is no spookier place to have one than an empty library after dark.

PREPARATION TIME

4 hours, plus 1 more hour if the golf variation is used

LENGTH OF PROGRAM

12 hours, or 5 hours for a shorter variation

NUMBER OF TEENS

25

SUGGESTED AGE RANGE

12–18 years

SHOPPING LIST

Food: pizza, either restaurant delivery or frozen; chips; popcorn; cookies; fruit or cut vegetables for snacking; soda; juice and donuts if teens will stay until morning

Board games if library does not have them already

Mini golf balls and clubs (plastic sets for small children usually available in summer)

Supplies for any additional activities and prizes for games (optional)

SETUP

Two to Three Weeks before Program

Write up and distribute permission slips, making it clear that teens will not be admitted into the lock-in without a signed slip. Make the due date for signed slips several days before the lock-in so you can prepare a list of registrants, control the number of participants, and not be faced with too many walk-ins. With the permission slips, send home a sheet of information that includes a list of things to bring, such as a sleeping bag, pillow, and the like.

Carefully plan where teens will be during the event. Depending on the size of the building, it may be a good idea to map out areas of activity. Will games go on throughout the entire library? Is there a quiet place for teens who actually want to sleep? Are there areas that are too private? If any teens are driving, do police need to be notified about cars? Provide a secure place for teens to put their personal belongings when they come in.

MAKE IT HAPPEN

Offer a range of activities that will keep all participants interested and engaged, whether in small, special-interest groups or in a single large group.

Pizza with a variety of toppings is a perfect first snack. Keep chips, popcorn, and cookies on hand for later in the evening. Make lots of soda available as well as fruit juice, water, coffee, and tea. For the morning, donuts and orange juice work well.

Movies	Select a variety of movies that will appeal to a variety of interests and keep them running all night. This will take care of plenty of teens. Some will come and go, and others may be happy to spend most or all of the night.
Ghost Hunt in the Library	Around midnight, take the group on a walk around the library, with all the lights off. Give adults flashlights, and tell a ghost story along the way. Have one or two helpers hide and make noise at certain places. Be careful not to get too creepy because if kids run screaming through a dark library, they could get hurt, or at the least, tear the place up.
Board Games	Provide a tub of games for the teens, such as Monopoly, chess, and checkers. This will provide a breather for you, and for the kids.
Golf in the Library?	Because it is irreverent and crazy, having a mini-golf course in the library during the lock-in is a great activity for teens. Equipment is actually simple to assemble: all you need are mallets, balls, score sheets, and course markers/holes. Amy used foam pool toys for mallets, which made the game really hard one year, but kiddie mini-golf mallets can generally be found at discount stores at the beginning of the warm season. Lightweight balls of any kind are fine. There are no rules about traditional sizes here. For course markers, the crazier the better! Though markers can be made on a computer, they may not survive eager play. Stand up books in V shapes to capture balls. Amy has also used the dollhouse and trains from the youth services area. Paperbacks and graphic novels make especially good ramps, too. Be creative. Traveling through many departments is fun but will prolong the game. Create nine holes with markers for starting points and holes. Draw a map for yourself because the course may get changed by enthusiastic players.
Other Activities	Almost any activity can be coupled with the lock-in. Henna painting (see July programs), tarot readings (see August programs), and journal writing are safe bets and not too much extra work.
Helpful Hints	Recruit as many adult volunteers as possible, so, if necessary, you can sleep in rotation. A good ratio is one adult for every five teens, but always have at least two adults. The kids will definitely be staying up all night.
	In almost all cases preapproval from your library administrator is necessary.
	Notify the closest police station about your event so they know there are people in the building. Ask them to do periodic drive-bys to check on you.
	Make sure the teens know they will not be admitted past the starting time and cannot leave until a parent comes to pick them up.

JUNE PASSIVE PROGRAMS

Ultimate TV Challenge. Make a poster with TV stars and have teens name the star and the character he or she played. You can do this on a theme, like stars named Bob, or classic TV stars, or singing TV stars. If no one on the staff can identify them, you will know that they will be a hit with the teens!

Bored Games. Set out three popular board games and make a chart for tracking high scores. Have teens enter their winning scores or the shortest times needed to win. Encourage groups coming in each day to try to beat the posted scores by playing the games themselves.

JUNE RESOURCES

Tie-Dyeing

Display Ideas
Tie-dyed T-shirts

Avedon, Richard, and Doon Arbus. *The Sixties.* New York: Random House, 1989.

Bleikorn, Samantha. *The Mini Mod Sixties Book.* San Francisco: Last Gasp, 2002.

Brachman, Wayne Harley. *Retro Desserts: Totally Hip, Updated Classic Desserts from the '40s, '50s, '60s, and '70s.* New York: Morrow, 2000.

Cain, Chelsea, ed. *Wild Child: Girlhoods in the Counterculture.* Foreword by Moon Zappa. Seattle: Seal Press, 1999.

Daniel, David. *White Rabbit.* New York: Thomas Dunne Books/St. Martin's Minotaur, 2003.

Didion, Joan. *Slouching towards Bethlehem.* New York: Modern Library, 2000.

Graham, Rosemary. *My Not-So-Terrible Time at Hippie Hotel.* New York: Viking, 2003.

Lifton, Betty Jean, and Thomas C. Fox. *Children of Vietnam.* New York: Atheneum, 1972.

O'Neil, Doris C. *Life—The '60s.* Introduction by Tom Brokaw. Boston: Little, Brown, 1989.

Owen, Cheryl, and Anna Murray. *The Grolier Kidscrafts Craft Book.* Danbury, CT: Grolier Educational, 1997.

Smith, Wes. *The Pied Pipers of Rock 'n' Roll: Radio Deejays of the 50s and 60s.* Marietta, GA: Longstreet, 1989.

Turbulent Years: The 60s. Alexandria, VA: Time-Life Books, 1998.

Overnight Fun

Pike, Christopher. *Slumber Party*. New York: Scholastic, 1985.

Schwartz, Alvin. *Scary Stories to Tell in the Dark*. New York: Harper and Row, 1986.

Traig, Jennifer. *Slumber Parties: Things to Make and Do*. San Francisco: Chronicle, 2002.

Wallace, Rich. *Restless: A Ghost's Story*. New York: Viking, 2003.

Whitney, Brooks. *Super Slumber Parties*. Middleton, WI: Pleasant Company, 1997.

Young, Richard, and Judy Dockrey. *Favorite Scary Stories of American Children*. Little Rock, AR: August House, 1999.

Display Ideas

S'mores makers, golf clubs and golf balls, pillows

July

Summer reading is in full swing, and plenty of time stretches in front of teens in July. Keep the momentum going with some fun summer programs. A few possible outdoor programs are outlined here, including a band night and a barbecue, but there are also indoor ideas such as henna painting. An effective way to tie in the entire community to summer teen events is through a Community Teen Appreciation Week. These are all great ways to attract teens into the library!

Barbecue

A barbecue at the library? Are we kidding? Seriously, having a summer barbecue is possible and fun, even indoors! Amy used to have a summer dance and realized that no boys would attend anything with *dance* in the title. So the same event was retitled as a barbecue with much more success. Teens even seemed more relaxed. At a dance they might be expected to dance or behave in ways that call attention to themselves, but at a barbecue they could simply eat and relax, even if there was a DJ and dancing.

PREPARATION TIME	2 hours plus research time
LENGTH OF PROGRAM	2–3 hours
NUMBER OF TEENS	40–60
SUGGESTED AGE RANGE	Grades 7–12

SHOPPING LIST	Food: hot dogs and burgers, buns and condiments, salad or cut veggies and fruit, french fries or chips and pretzels, canned soda, cookies or brownies (optional)
	Paper goods: tablecloths, plates, napkins, and cups
	Cooler for soda
	Several small prizes and one large prize for drawings

SETUP

Three to Six Months before Program

Investigate the food and DJ availability in your area. If you or other staff will be cooking the food, find out the lowest prices in your area for burgers and hot dogs. If you are having the program indoors, find out how much it would cost to get hot dogs ready-made from a restaurant. Amy had a hot dog vendor come in with his cart and go up the library elevator when it rained the night of her first barbecue. It was such a hit that the event is held indoors every year now. Many more teens were comfortable dancing indoors, in an enclosed space, rather than in the outdoor library amphitheater where anyone could see them. Planning ahead allows time to solicit possible donations from restaurants and grocery stores.

It can be tricky to work with DJs: (1) they are expensive and (2) due to controversial lyrics, many do not carry the rap music or popular hits that teens like to listen to. Or sometimes even worse, they carry all the hot music with the uncensored lyrics. Different ethnic groups may have preferences about music as well. It is crucial to get input from your teen advisory board, high school students, and other teens about what is popular. The high school may be able to direct you to DJs they use or to students who are DJs on the side. Teens like to see someone close to their age as a DJ whenever possible.

One Month before Program

Put posters everywhere for this one—pools, high schools where summer classes are held, and anywhere that donated or sold you food for the program.

This type of program attracts more participants as a drop-in activity, but registration helps with food ordering. Offer teens who register ahead of time a bonus raffle ticket.

One Week before Program

Confirm any ordered food and the DJ, including the setup time. It is worth it to pay the DJ for an extra half hour of setup time to ensure that the program will start on time. Plan on having drawings periodically or dance contests like the limbo to keep the teens involved, even if some do not participate.

Two Hours before Program

The first year Amy held a summer dance, it was entitled "Dance of the Decades," complete with lots of sixties decorations, costumes, and the like. Very few teens came because it was just too complicated. Simple red and white checked tablecloths on the food tables and red and white paper products can serve as decorations for this event. Having it outdoors may necessitate citronella candles.

Have a prominent box for the raffle slips. Have staff members posted near the entrances to the event with slips of paper on which teens can write names. Include space for addresses if teens want to be included on the mailing list.

MAKE IT HAPPEN   The barbecue is an easy program to involve both junior and senior high school students. If it is going to be held for junior high students only, plan more activities, such as a potato chip tasting contest (see next section). High school students are less self-conscious about hanging out, yet are still somewhat shy about dancing, so be sure to offer some line dances that everyone knows, including the electric slide. High school students can be very opinionated about their tastes in music, which will require a DJ who can offer plenty of age-appropriate variety. Putting games such as mancala, Sorry, chess, checkers, and cards at some of the tables is also a good idea for shy teens.

Extra Activities   *Potato Chip Tasting.* Buy unusual flavors and colors of potato chips and put them in numbered bowls on a table. Give teens pencils and paper or forms to write what flavor they think is in each bowl.

Pie-Eating Contest. See how fast contestants can eat a pie with hands tied behind their backs rather than how many pies they can eat.

Limbo Contest. This is always a good dance-floor ice-breaker.

Incentives. Award simple, fun prizes for rapping, break-dancing, and other activities on the dance floor to encourage more teens to join in. Cool key chains and candy bars make good prizes.

Water Balloon Toss. Outside only.

Battle of the Bands

Who says a library has to be a quiet place all the time? A battle of the bands is a sure-fire program to liven things up and bring out your inner DJ. Teens with bands have very few places to play for an audience. They will jump at the chance to play for their friends and family at your library. In fact, by the time they have spread the word around school, your publicity will be pretty much taken care of.

PREPARATION TIME   8–10 hours planning, plus 2 hours setup

LENGTH OF PROGRAM   3 hours (4 bands each playing for 30 minutes plus 3 15-minute intermissions for switching bands will allow 15 minutes or so at the end for time overruns, prizes, and thank-yous)

NUMBER OF TEENS	4 bands and up to 100 teens if outside, 50–100 teens inside, if space is available
SUGGESTED AGE RANGE	12–18 years
SHOPPING LIST	Food: water for bands; soft drinks, chips, and cookies for audience (pizza, sandwiches, or hot dogs optional)
	Balloons or bubbles, multicolored string lights
	Extension cords (depending on distance from stage to library)
	5 surge protectors (minimum)
	Prizes or certificates (optional, but could include gift certificates to music or electronics stores)

SETUP

One Month before Program

To recruit bands to play at the event put together posters and flyers advertising the Battle of the Bands. Send them to local schools, music shops, and teen centers, and place them throughout the library. Include contact information, available time slots, and other key facts.

To publicize the event, revise the posters and flyers by adding the names of the bands performing and the times at which they are playing. Be sure to emphatically state the age range of attendees you will allow into the program.

Performing in front of a real audience will be a first for some of the bands, so help them out a little by making it a learning experience. Teens need to know what to expect the library to provide and what is expected of them. Write up a contract that spells out agreements regarding time slots (everyone wants to play last!), places to store equipment, rules of conduct, who will provide extension cords, and so on. (See the sample band contract in the appendix.) Make sure all members of each band sign one copy for you to keep at the library and one copy of their own. At the bottom of the contract, require the names of all band members and their contact information, in case you need to contact them.

Solicit at least three volunteer judges from local radio stations, music stores, or staff.

Two Weeks before Program

For a large event like this, plan on having a number of staff members and teen volunteers present. Organize and confirm their participation at least two weeks prior to the program. Ask one staff member or teen to be the MC for the evening. This person will introduce each band, signal band members if they run over time, and announce the winning band at the end. It is a good idea to call the bands and confirm their participation as well.

One or Two Days before Program

Decorations for this event can range from the pretty simple to the really extravagant. All you really need is a stage area, dancing space, and dim lights. To really get things going, set up one or two refreshment tables with tablecloths and centerpieces. Blowing up a few balloons and hanging them from the ceiling or around the doors is a nice touch. Or you can go all out and hang multicolored light strings, lava lamps, black lights, and so forth. Colored lightbulbs are great replacements for regular bulbs to help set the mood. Set up a stage if your library does not already have one or if your event will be held outdoors. You can use something as simple as sheets of plywood, or you can rent a stage from a local rental store. If the program will be indoors, find an area with a wide-open space, as in an auditorium, where the stage area is pretty much prearranged. Make sure there are available outlets, appropriate extension cords, and surge protectors that are able to handle heavy electrical currents.

Day of Program

Water is a must for the band members. If you have the space, create a private green room for performers set up with water, other beverages, and snacks. Having soda, potato chips, and cookies out on trays should be sufficient for the bands and the audience. Pizza, sandwiches, and hot dogs all are teen-friendly foods that are great for this event, if you want to get more elaborate.

Staff members will want to know what is going on with all that noise! Make sure to send a letter out to the staff concerning the possible volume-control issues, and if necessary, run through a sound check beforehand to ensure that the noise will not get out of hand. It is also a good idea to notify local authorities (police, chamber of commerce) and neighborhood groups if you are having your event outside.

MAKE IT HAPPEN

As audience members arrive, have staff or teen volunteers show them where refreshments, washrooms, and seating can be found for the evening. If the program is outdoors, teens can sit on the ground, bring chairs, or stand and listen to bands or dance as they do at concerts.

Between sets, teens can mingle and enjoy the refreshments. You can also use that time for announcements and reminders or play music from a CD player.

When the last band has played, give the judges up to fifteen minutes if they need it to choose which band played best. (Staff and judges should decide in advance if popularity with the audience will be a factor in awarding prizes.) When the winning band has been chosen, the MC can make the announcement and award the prizes.

Henna Painting

The henna plant is one of the oldest sources of cosmetics ever used and is extremely safe. In many cultures, beautiful henna decorations adorn hands for special events. Natural henna, when applied to the skin, rarely causes any adverse reactions. If you are concerned, you should do a small patch test first. Natural henna is safe even for use on children, as it contains no dangerous chemical dyes or harsh additives.

PREPARATION TIME 5 hours

LENGTH OF PROGRAM 1½ hours

NUMBER OF TEENS 25

SUGGESTED AGE RANGE 11–18 years

SHOPPING LIST
Food: hummus, pita bread, yogurt, dates, almonds, and the like

Small plastic sandwich bags

Small squeeze bottles

Needle to poke holes in sandwich bags or bottles

3 ounces of henna (black or green, available online or at local health food stores)

Alcohol wipes

Soap

Sponges

Newspapers to cover floor and table

Black tea bags

Concentrated lemon juice

Sitar music (optional)

SETUP

One Day before Program

Most local health food stores and some grocery and beauty stores sell henna mixes or you can mix your own. Below is one recipe to help get you started, but if you consult books and Internet sites, you may find recipes that will last longer or shorter, depending on the result you want. The following recipe should work for one person:

1. Boil 1½ cups of water.
2. Place 3 tablespoons of henna mix into a glass or metal cup or a bowl.
3. In a separate cup or bowl, pour the boiling water over 2 teabags.
4. Let the tea sit for just about 10 minutes.
5. Add 5 tablespoons of freshly squeezed lemon juice or premixed lemon concentrate.
6. Slowly add the tea and lemon mix to the henna, bit by bit.

7. Mix thoroughly until the mixture reaches the consistency of toothpaste.

8. Let your mixture sit out for around 2–4 hours or overnight, covered with plastic wrap or in a covered container.

9. You are now ready to paint!

Spoon the paste into an art bottle or a plastic sandwich bag with a needle-sized hole poked into one corner.

Day of Program

Set up tables with brightly colored silklike tablecloths covering them. Sprinkle fake flower petals over them. Cover the floor around each table with paper. Sitar music playing softly in the background and maybe a little incense burning in a corner will help set the mood. To apply the dye, gather art bottles or other bottles with small tips, or use a needle to poke a small hole in a number of plastic sandwich bags. This activity can get pretty messy, so it is a good idea to have a sink nearby or to have soap, water, and sponges handy.

Since henna painting has its origins in Africa, Asia, and the Middle East, make this a multicultural event. For refreshments, hummus and pita bread, yogurt and dried fruits (especially dates and figs), or even rice pudding are excellent choices that can be prepared easily or purchased inexpensively. Spiced teas, fruit juices, or small samples of coconut milk make great beverages.

MAKE IT HAPPEN

There are a variety of books with henna patterns in them, if you do not consider yourself artistic. Otherwise, you can make up your own patterns. Look for inspiration in any book you want, such as nature books and art books. For best results, draw or trace a design on the skin first and then cover it with henna.

Henna painting is a great way to get kids interested in art and can be a helpful springboard for learning about other cultures. Make sure to do some background research on henna painting and how it is traditionally used, and share your findings with the participants. Inviting a native of India or another Asian or Middle Eastern country to speak and demonstrate will help make this a really fun program, and interesting, too.

Helpful Hints

Make sure the area of the skin is clean and dry before applying the henna. This lets your design show up clearer and last longer.

If you want the henna darker, keep it on as long as you can.

JULY PASSIVE PROGRAMS

Toon Up the Heat. Have teens match descriptions of cartoon characters to their names or the names of comic strips to the years they were first drawn.

Hot, Hot, Hot. Put a map of the fifty states on a sheet of paper with a list of ten record high temperatures. Have teens match each hottest known temperature to the correct state.

JULY RESOURCES

Summertime

Display Ideas
Beach balls, toy barbecue food or toy grill, barbecue cooking tools, bottle of sunscreen, sunglasses, fold-up camp chairs, flip-flops

Benduhn, Tea. *Gravel Queen*. New York: Simon and Schuster Books for Young Readers, 2003.

Cann, Kate. *Grecian Holiday*. New York: Avon, 1999.

Clark, Catherine. *Frozen Rodeo*. New York: HarperCollins, 2003.

Dessen, Sarah. *The Truth about Forever*. New York: Viking, 2004.

Donnelly, Jennifer. *A Northern Light*. Orlando, FL: Harcourt, 2003.

Gauthier, Gail. *Saving the Planet and Stuff*. New York: G. P. Putnam's Sons, 2003.

Glick, Susan. *One Shot*. New York: Henry Holt, 2003.

Lubar, David. *Dunk*. New York: Clarion, 2002.

Mosier, Elizabeth. *My Life as a Girl*. New York: Random House, 1999.

Paulsen, Gary. *The Beet Fields: Memories of a Sixteenth Summer*. New York: Delacorte, 2000.

Rock Star Reads

Anderson, Stephen. *So You Wanna Be a Rockstar? How to Create Music, Get Gigs, and Maybe Even Make It Big*. Hillsboro, OR: Beyond Words, 1999.

Bell, Madison Smartt. *Anything Goes*. New York: Pantheon, 2002.

Bozza, Anthony. *Whatever You Say I Am: The Life and Times of Eminem*. New York: Crown, 2003.

Brewster, Bill, and Frank Broughton. *Last Night a DJ Saved My Life*. New York: Grove, 2000.

Carlson, Melody. *Sold Out*. Sisters, OR: Multnomah, 2003.

Corbet, Robert. *Fifteen Love*. New York: Walker, 2003.

Crouch, Tanja L. *One Hundred Careers in the Music Business*. Hauppauge, NY: Barron's, 2001.

Dessen, Sarah. *This Lullaby*. New York: Viking, 2002.

Fleischmann, Paul. *Breakout*. Chicago: Cricket, 2003.

Fricke, Jim, and Charlie Ahearn. *Yes Yes Y'all: The Experience Music Project Oral History of Hip-Hop's First Decade.* Cambridge, MA: Da Capo, 2002.

Going, K. L. *Fat Kid Rules the World.* New York: G. P. Putnam's Sons, 2003.

Greenberg, Keith Elliot. *Heavy Metal.* Minneapolis: Lerner, 1986.

Hoggarth, Janet. *Create Your Own Girl Band.* New York: Scholastic, 2001.

Hoye, Jacob, and Karolyn Ali. *Tupac: Resurrection, 1971–1996.* New York: Atria, 2003.

Johnson, Jeff. *Careers for Music Lovers and Other Tuneful Types.* Lincolnwood, IL: VGM Career Horizons, 1997.

Kennedy, Pagan. *The Exes.* New York: Scribner Paperback Fiction, 1999.

Malone, Bonz, Nichole Beattie, and DJ Lindy. *Hip Hop Immortals.* New York: Thunder's Mouth, 2003.

Morse, Tim. *Classic Rock Stories: The Stories behind the Greatest Songs of All Time.* New York: St. Martin's Griffin, 1998.

Reighley, Kurt B. *Looking for the Perfect Beat: The Art and Culture of the DJ.* New York: Pocket Books, 2000.

Henna Painting

Batra, Sumita. *The Art of Mehndi.* New York: Penguin Studio, 1999.

English, Karen. *Nadia's Hands.* Honesdale, PA: Boyds Mills 1999.

Gilbert, Derrick I. M. *HennaMan: Poems.* New York: Riverhead, 2000.

Hidier, Tanuja Desai. *Born Confused.* New York: Scholastic, 2002.

Miller, Jean-Chris. *The Body Art Book: A Complete, Illustrated Guide to Tattoos, Piercings, and Other Body Modifications.* New York: Berkley, 1997.

Ritz, David. *Tattoo Nation: Portraits of Celebrity Body Art.* Boston: Bulfinch, 2002.

Staples, Suzanne Fisher. *Haveli.* New York: Random House, 1995.

———. *Shiva's Fire.* Thorndike, ME: Thorndike Press, 2000.

van den Beukel, Dorine. *Traditional Mehndi Designs: A Treasury of Henna Body Art.* Boston: Shambhala Press, 2000.

Vijayaraghavan, Vineeta. *Motherland.* New York: Soho, 2001.

Wilkinson, Beth. *Coping with the Dangers of Tattooing, Body Piercing, and Branding.* New York: Rosen, 1998.

August

Summer is winding down, but there is still time for a few fun programs. As teens think about the next school year and about choices for their future, the Who Are You? program will fit in with discussion of personalities. Get teen girls geared up for fall with a Back-to-School Fashion Show. Then get the teen area of the library ready for a new school year by having teens design colorful murals.

Who Are You? Tarot, Fortunes, and More

So much of teen life involves thinking about the future that it is no wonder that they are often interested in tarot, palm reading, and other methods of fortune-telling. This program offers teens a chance to sample different methods of looking into the future in a fun, festive manner.

PREPARATION TIME	3 hours, including room setup
LENGTH OF PROGRAM	1½ hours
NUMBER OF TEENS	30
SUGGESTED AGE RANGE	11–18 years
SHOPPING LIST	Food: iced tea, lemonade, cookies Confetti

Colored fabric

Candles

Runes

Ouija board

SETUP

Two to Three Weeks before Program

Plan to set up tables for a variety of activities, and designate a staff member to run each one. Some suggestions are palm reading, runes reading, Ouija board, tarot reading, astrology, and numerology. Check out a book on one of the subjects, and do a little light reading. Encourage staff members who will be running tables to do the same. In each field, there are simple enough activities that even people who are not experts can do them.

Day of Program

Some party stores sell confetti in the shapes of the zodiac signs. If you can, buy this to sprinkle on top of the tables. On each table, drape colored fabrics and set a lighted candle. Allot one table to each activity, that is, one for palm reading, one for astrology, one for tarot, and so on. Give the beverages and refreshments mystical titles. For example, you could follow a zodiac theme, if you wanted, and serve Taurus tea, Libra lemonade, and so forth.

MAKE IT HAPPEN

As teens arrive, invite them to tour the different tables of activities. Some activities, such as a Ouija board, can run themselves, but runes reading, palm reading, tarot cards, astrology, and numerology need to be done by staff members. Have a few chairs at each table so teens can listen to others' experiences if they are shy about trying things themselves. Create a handout that asks teens what lucky objects they have, what their zodiac sign is, and other potentially useful questions about themselves. Place the handout and pencils on a table near the door so that teens may pick them up as they enter. Teens can carry their handouts from table to table to record anything interesting they hear, and staff can consult the handouts for information that will help with the readings.

It is a good idea to have some tables with chairs in the middle of the room stocked with board games that teens may play while waiting for their turn at an activity. These could include games about future plans like Life, or mind-reading like Battleship, or even Magic 8 Ball.

Make a display of books on fortune-telling and the activities demonstrated during the program that teens may check out as they leave.

Back-to-School Fashion Show

Make the library a scene for a fun, funky fashion show. Clothing is important to teens, especially at back-to-school time. Many areas of the country do not have a large mall nearby where teens can see a professional show, so they will really enjoy this experience.

How many stores participate and how much clothing is available will dictate how long the show will be, but have at least enough material to fill thirty to forty-five minutes. This program should draw a large number of participants, both as models and as audience members.

PREPARATION TIME	10 hours
LENGTH OF PROGRAM	1½ hours
NUMBER OF TEENS	50–100 in audience
SUGGESTED AGE RANGE	11–18 years
SHOPPING LIST	Food: cookies, chips, dip, raw vegetables, cheese, lemonade, soda, bottled water
	Small paper plates, cups, and paper napkins

SETUP

Three Months before Program

Preparation for this program needs to begin at least three months in advance to provide enough time to coordinate clothes, models, and other key elements.

Create flyers and a sign-up sheet at the library advertising the need for teens to model at this event. Include the event's date and time, details of required practice sessions, and other important information about the commitment of time and energy expected of models.

One Month before Program

Visit managers of local clothing stores at least thirty days in advance to explain the event and solicit outfits to borrow and showcase. As you leave, give each manager a letter that summarizes the information you presented. Avoid contacting large corporations like Sears and American Eagle because they will probably be more reticent to help out. Look for small, independently owned, trendy local businesses and thrift stores aimed at the younger crowd. Their fashions will have greater appeal, and chances are that they will be more eager for free advertising opportunities. To simplify organization, minimize the number of retailers involved and, if possible, try to recruit a single well-stocked merchandiser to sponsor the entire show.

Some stores prefer that the models come in to try items on so they can put together the perfect outfit for each individual. Other stores already have outfits in mind and prefer to work from a list of models and their sizes. Either way, the models need to try the clothes on well before the show. As soon as your list of models is complete, call the store managers to let them know how many models will be stopping by, to set up a convenient time for the models to come, and to find out any other preferences or concerns the managers might have.

To keep the clothes clean and safe, leave them at the store until a day or two before the event, depending on when your dress rehearsal will be held.

Two Weeks before Program

Follow up with phone calls to store managers at least two weeks before the event. Make sure to keep an annotated list of which clothing items come from each store and which models will be wearing them. Use the list to create a script that briefly describes each outfit and identifies the model who is wearing it.

Select books to promote during the fashion show. Choose one book for each model to carry, and write out a short description of it to include in your script. When reading the description of an outfit, include a segue to the book. For example, "And Stacy is holding Tanjua Desai Hidier's *Born Confused.* . . ." If possible, find books that coordinate with the outfits and outfits that coordinate with the books. Print out a list of stores, outfits, books, and models for audience members.

Have each model sign a contract specifying the rules of the fashion show, the person in charge, responsibility for each outfit, and the like. Invite a local pageant participant or organizer to visit with your models and teach them how to stand, walk the runway, pose, and show off their clothing and accessories.

Hold at least two rehearsals to make sure that clothes fit, that models know when to enter and exit as well as how and where to walk, that the script works, and that things in general will go smoothly.

Set check-in time for at least one hour before the show to allow plenty of time for getting ready and dealing with unforeseen circumstances.

One or Two Days before Program

Ask two or more adults to pick up the clothing from the merchants on the day of the dress rehearsal. Depending on the amount of clothing and the number of merchants, you may need more than one team. The volunteers and each store manager should together make a list of everything that is leaving the store. Then, when they return the clothing, the volunteers and the store managers should use the lists to check each item coming back.

Day of Program

Setup on the day of the program will take at least two hours, and you will need help for setting up furniture, the runway, the refreshment table, and all. Arrange rows of chairs to seat up to one hundred people, depending on the crowd you expect. Make sure there is an entrance from the dressing room and space for the runway in front of the chairs. Tape Xs on the floor or the stage at each spot you want the models to stop and turn. The narrator will have worked on pacing during rehearsals and should have the updated script with the exact clothing information now as well. Set up a simple sound system, with a microphone for the moderator and a CD player and speakers for background music.

Set up a table at the back of the room, with simple, noncrumbly refreshments. This is for the fashion show's audience. Cookies on a platter, chips with dip, and a vegetable and cheese tray should work well. Lemonade, water, and soda will suffice for beverages.

MAKE IT HAPPEN Staff and volunteers will need to be on hand to supervise the models. All models should remain backstage until the end of the show to ensure the safety of the outfits. Ideally, you should have at least three helpers with the models, two to greet guests, and two at the refreshment table.

When audience members arrive, have music playing. Have teen volunteers pass out programs and direct people to their seats and the refreshment table. Once most of the audience has arrived, a teen volunteer should signal the narrator to begin the show.

Helpful Hints Keep very careful records of every item of clothing, including where it came from, who will wear it, when it needs to be returned, and other useful details.

Make sure the models do not get anywhere near the food. They are going to want to eat, but insist they wait until after they have changed back into their own clothes. If the borrowed clothing should get stained and ruined, the library will be held responsible.

Invite local beauty businesses to participate by donating facials, makeovers, or other indulgences to the models or to be used as prizes. Make sure that donors are acknowledged at the show.

Invite teens to make and model their own clothes or to put their own outfits together if you have trouble obtaining enough garments from merchants.

Decorateens

A space that has wonderful, peer-made art is especially appealing to teens. Many libraries cannot afford to spend a lot of money decorating a designated teen area. Presenting a series of programs that focus on creating decorative art will give teens ownership in their area and produce an inexpensive yet priceless set of decorations for any library. This activity is adapted from programs at several libraries that have been transformed through teen art.

PREPARATION TIME 1 hour

LENGTH OF PROGRAM 4 hours

NUMBER OF TEENS 25

SUGGESTED AGE RANGE	Grades 6–12
SHOPPING LIST	Food: pizza, chips, beverages
	Large pieces of felt for background plus heavy felt for cutout pieces, or heavy butcher paper for paper murals
	Rubber cement and glue
	Very sharp scissors, one pair for each teen
SETUP	This program will involve lots of planning to achieve a pleasing result. A local artist who is talented as well as successful in working with teens may be enlisted to help.
Two Months before Program	Hold an initial planning meeting with staff, the artist, and a regular teen group, such as a teen advisory board. Brainstorm design ideas and colors and decide what story the banners or murals will tell or what idea they will convey.
One Month before Program	Ask the artist to join the teens in looking around the library to get ideas and images. The TAB members involved with the design of the banners can begin recruiting other teens to attend the program at which the banners will actually be made.
Two Weeks before Program	Purchase supplies and have the artist begin to design some basic shapes for each banner or mural, to be embellished and added to by the teens at the event. The banners or murals will take up a great deal of space and will need to dry, so think carefully about location for this program.
Day of Program	Lay out the felt backdrops and the precut felt figurative elements, such as figures and symbols from the artist. The artist should guide the teens in choosing all colors and elements. Having pieces cut ahead of time will ensure that the workshop activities will be organized and that the banners will be completed. Everyone can then enjoy the process and not feel rushed for time.
MAKE IT HAPPEN	When teens arrive, they will find the felt backdrops laid out with the precut felt elements. Some teens can apply the precut figures to the background with rubber cement while others can draw additional smaller pieces or embellish precut shapes. For example, when this program was done for the Allen County Public Library in Indiana, the "Sports" banner contained a football, but it was hard to tell what it was, so a teen made it more distinctive by cutting out felt lacings and gluing them on.
	Paper murals could be painted in a similar way. A library with enough funds could work with local art departments and use canvas and paints to create more professional and durable decorations.

Serving pizza, chips, and beverages when the murals are finished will help reward the teens for their efforts and may even attract additional teens to the program.

AUGUST RESOURCES

Fortune-Telling

Display Ideas
Magic 8 Ball, tarot cards, Ouija board

Abadie, M. J. *The Everything Tarot Book.* Holbrook, MA: Adams Media, 1999.

———. *Teen Astrology: The Ultimate Guide to Making Your Life Your Own.* Rochester, VT: Bindu, 2001.

Fontana, David. *The Secret Language of Symbols: A Visual Key to Symbols and Their Meanings.* New York: Chronicle, 1994.

Gravelle, Karen. *Five Ways to Know about You.* New York: Walker, 2002.

Hazel, Peter. *Palmistry: Quick and Easy.* St. Paul, MN: Llewellyn, 2001.

Macgregor, Rob, and Megan Macgregor. *Star Power: Astrology for Teens.* Franklin Lakes, NJ: New Page, 2003.

Pollack, Rachel. *Complete Illustrated Guide to Tarot.* New York: Gramercy, 2004.

Renee, Janina. *Tarot Spells.* St. Paul, MN: Llewellyn, 2000.

Shaw, Maria. *Tarot Kit for Teens.* St. Paul, MN: Llewellyn, 2004.

Webster, Richard. *Palm Reading for Beginners: Find Your Future in the Palm of Your Hand.* St. Paul, MN: Llewellyn, 2000.

Fashion

Bird, Eugenie. *Fairie-ality: The Fashion Collection from the House of Ellwand.* Cambridge, MA: Candlewick, 2002.

Knowles, Tina. *Destiny's Style: Bootylicious Fashion, Beauty, and Lifestyle Secrets from Destiny's Child.* New York: HarperCollins, 2002.

Levine, Malcolm, and Kate Mayfield. *10 Steps to Fashion Freedom: Discover Your Personal Style from the Inside Out.* New York: Crown, 2001.

Weil, Christa. *Secondhand Chic: Finding Fabulous Fashion at Vintage, Consignment, and Thrift Shops.* New York: Pocket Books, 1999.

West, Tracy. *Say My Name: A Guide to Fashion Tees.* New York: Grosset and Dunlap, 2002.

Banner and Mural Designs

Harms, Carol Jean. *Quick and Easy Banner Designs.* St. Louis: Concordia, 1996.

Hazelwood, Robin. *An Introduction to Drawing: An Artist's Guide to Skills and Techniques.* Cincinnati: North Light, 2004.

Litherland, Janet. *The Complete Banner Handbook: A Creative Guide for Banner Design and Construction.* Colorado Springs, CO: Meriwether, 1987.

Muehlenhardt, Amy. *Drawing and Learning about Cars: Using Shapes and Lines.* Minneapolis: Picture Window, 2004.

Sidaway, Ian. *How to Draw Still Life: A Set-by-Step Guide for Beginners with Ten Projects.* London: New Holland, 2003.

Thomson, Ruth. *Creatures.* Langhorne, PA: Chelsea Clubhouse, 2004.

Znamierowski, Alfred. *World Encyclopedia of Flags: The Definitive Guide to International Flags, Banners, Standards, and Ensigns.* New York: Lorenz, 1999.

September

Teens are busier than ever as school returns to session. As a result, teen attendance at the library in September may be slow. There are still some appropriate programs for this month, however. It is the perfect time for Library Survivor, a scavenger hunt designed to remind teens about what the library has to offer them. Teens could also start getting geared up for October with a Scary Story Contest that could begin in September and continue into October.

Scary Story Contest

A good program that is not strictly for Halloween is a Scary Story Contest. Some areas do not celebrate Halloween, but horror and fantasy themes are often popular with teens, so this writing contest can cover a variety of interests at this time of year. A general writing contest is often too broad and daunting for some teens, so writing on a single theme should be attractive, especially with enough marketing. Another variation on the horror theme is "It's Alive," as used for the 2004 Teen Read Week. In this writing contest, teens are asked to describe an inanimate object that comes alive. While this section focuses on the scary story idea, "It's Alive" could easily be substituted.

PREPARATION TIME	4 hours
LENGTH OF PROGRAM	1 month
NUMBER OF TEENS	25–40

SUGGESTED AGE RANGE   Grades 7–12

SHOPPING LIST   Items are similar to those for the April poetry contest:

> Prizes for winners, possibly to be purchased after seeing how many students enter
>
> Small tokens of appreciation with a scary theme, such as eyeballs, pencils, and candy, for judges and for teachers of participants
>
> Optional incentive prize, such as an autographed book or a journal, for the teacher or class with the most entries

SETUP   The planning and implementation of the Scary Story Contest will follow the pattern of the April Poetry Contest fairly closely because many of the rules and procedures will be similar. Please consult the description of the April contest for both general and specific suggestions about planning and implementation, and adapt them to your situation.

As with the other writing contests in this book, the advance preparation allows adequate time for marketing. Given that the fall is a very busy time for teens, it is a good idea to begin letting teachers and media librarians know about the contest right when school begins, in late August or early September. Bring handouts and flyers about the contest to all the back-to-school functions you are invited to, such as parents' nights.

Teachers and teens will forget about the program if too much time elapses between the initial publicity and the announcement of winners. If the handouts are available beginning in late August, winners' names should be revealed in mid-October at the latest. If entries are due by October 1, this allows a couple of weeks for judging and posting. Be sure to specify when winners will be disclosed and how, whether by poster within the library, through announcements at schools, or on the library website. Be sure that the nonwinners' letters have arrived by the time that the winners are posted. Consider patterning this letter after the nonwinners' letter for the April Poetry Contest (see appendix).

Because the Scary Story Contest runs at the beginning of school year, the solicitation of entries may require extra effort. Even if you distribute handouts and flyers at every opportunity in the library, the schools, parent-teacher meetings, teen centers, and the like, the contest may still get lost in the flurry of back-to-school activities. Thus, to build interest, send e-mails and snail mail to teens and teachers who participated in the spring poetry contest and other library-sponsored writing contests.

MAKE IT HAPPEN   If school has been in session several weeks but few entries have been submitted and few teachers have expressed interest, try to inspire creativity by sending booklists of scary stories to teachers and teens along with a reminder about the program.

While it is possible to set up the contest to include all students from twelve to eighteen years of age, it may be fairest to split the competition into two divisions, one for junior high schoolers and one for senior high schoolers. If some entries are illustrated or have a decorated cover, they could be put in a separate category.

Because judging a story-writing contest requires a big time commitment, it is OK if only twenty to thirty teens participate. It is important to read and judge the entries as they come in, though the bulk of them will be turned in on or near the deadline date, especially those from classes.

As with the poetry contest, stories should be published on websites or in print at the library, especially the winners. Winning entries may also be featured at the Little Coffee Shop of Horrors, a program recommended for October.

Library Survivor

Reality TV shows are a huge hit with teens everywhere. Playing Library Survivor is a great way to get teens involved in the library and acquaint them with the awesome resources available just for them. When teens explore their library using the scavenger hunt/survivor format, they also see firsthand how cool the library is (and how everyone can survive a trip there)!

PREPARATION TIME	1 hour
LENGTH OF PROGRAM	1½ hours
NUMBER OF TEENS	5 teams of 5 teens, or 25 total
SUGGESTED AGE RANGE	11–18 years
SHOPPING LIST	Food: bite-size candy bars (for all the players) and full-size candy bars (for the winning team) to be handed out at the end of the program
	Four different colors of paper
SETUP **One Day before Program**	Using one letter per piece of paper, spell out the words *Library*, *Survivor*, *Skills*, and *Winner*. For each word, use a different color of paper. Stick a gold star to one letter in each word.
	Create a survival guide that will lead teens through the game. Adapt the sample in the appendix to your specific library.

| One Hour before Program | About one hour before the event begins, send staff members throughout the library to hide the colored letters according to your survival guide answer sheet. The team with the most letters at the end of the hunt wins. |

MAKE IT HAPPEN

Library Survivor: Can YOU Survive?

Here are the directions for a sample survival guide from the Lawrence Public Library. The sample clue list is in the appendix, with answers shown in italics.

Directions: Letters spelling out LIBRARY SURVIVOR SKILLS WINNER are hidden all over the library. The object of the game is to find all the letters and learn about the awesome features the library has to offer.

Each team will be given a list of clues. Each clue will take you to a different feature of the library. Solve the clue, then find the place in question.

Each word is a different color. One letter in each word has a star on it. If you find one of those letters, your team can participate in an Immunity Challenge. If everyone on your team can name three new things they learned at the library today, your team will win the challenge and win immunity for the word in question. (Winning immunity for a word means that your team will receive credit for an entire word even if you are missing a few letters.)

Helpful Hints

Keep the team size to about five kids.

Give all teams the same clues but shuffle their order to ensure that all teams will not be in the same place at the same time.

As the event will be taking place while the library is open, it is a good idea to limit the noise, or patrons and staff will complain. To encourage the Survivor theme, tell the groups that making too much noise will get them kicked off the island.

SEPTEMBER PASSIVE PROGRAMS

Celebrate Banned Books Week. Create a puzzle sheet of scrambled titles (with a few clues) of the top ten banned books from the previous year. You can find the list at http://www.ala.org/ala/oif/bannedbooksweek/bannedbooksweek.htm. A variation of this would be to create a list of banned book titles and a list of reasons for banning and to ask teens to match each title to the reason it was banned. This will illustrate that many books are banned for the same reason.

Library Clue. Based on the game of Clue, invent a crime that takes place at the library and involves staff members or teen advisory board members. Use photos of the individuals and made-up names. Display a map of the library (real or imagined) and the photos along with the fictional scenario. Provide sheets listing the rooms, weapons, and suspects. Each week, release information that would eliminate some choices. Continue releasing information until the last week, when the entire murder scenario is revealed. This can also be done on the library website. As soon as teens think they know the solution, they can write it up and turn it in. Everyone who submits a solution will be entered in drawings for prizes.

There are many, many good scary stories and horror books. Some are more appropriate for older teens. Although you need to look at individual titles, the following authors have contributed some of the most popular works in this genre:

Joan Aiken	Annette Curtis Klause	Darren Shan
V. C. Andrews	Dean Koontz	R. L. Stine
Washington Irving	Edgar Allan Poe	
Stephen King	Anne Rice	

The authors and titles cited in the list below are also good for the Little Coffee Shop of Horrors, featured in October.

Atwater-Rhodes, Amelia. *In the Forests of the Night*. New York: Delacorte, 1999.

Bradbury, Ray. *Something Wicked This Way Comes*. New York: Bantam, 1962.

Shelley, Mary Wollstonecraft. *Frankenstein*. Various publishers and dates.

Stevenson, Robert Louis. *The Strange Case of Dr. Jekyll and Mr. Hyde*. Various publishers and dates.

Yolen, Jane. *Vampires: A Collection of Original Stories*. New York: HarperCollins, 1991.

Zindel, Paul. *The Doom Stone*. New York: HarperCollins, 1995.

Hidden Treasure and Survival Stories

Anderson, Janet. *The Last Treasure*. New York: Dutton's Children's Books, 2003.

Burgett, Gordon. *Treasure and Scavenger Hunts: How to Plan, Create, and Give Them*. Santa Maria, CA: Communications Unlimited, 1994.

Byars, Betsy. *The Seven Treasure Hunts*. New York: HarperCollins, 1991.

Clements, Bruce. *The Treasure of Plunderell Manor*. New York: Farrar, Straus and Giroux, 1987.

Donnelly, Judy. *True-Life Treasure Hunts*. New York: Random House, 1993.

Dowswell, Paul. *Tales of Real Survival*. Tulsa, OK: EDC, 1995.

Golden, Christopher. *Soul Survivor*. New York: Pocket Pulse, 1999.

Hamilton, Virginia. *The Mystery of Drear House: The Conclusion of the Dies Drear Chronicle*. New York: Greenwillow, 1987.

Kaniut, Larry. *Danger Stalks the Land: Alaskan Tales of Death and Survival*. New York: St. Martin's Griffin, 1999.

McMurtry, Ken. *Beware the Snake's Venom*. Milwaukee: Gareth Stevens, 1996.

Twain, Mark. *The Adventures of Tom Sawyer*. Cutchogue, NY: Buccaneer, 1976.

October

October is a great time for people working with teens. In addition to Teen Read Week to celebrate, there is Halloween. Some communities may not celebrate Halloween, but many teens like horror, mystery, and fantasy, so highlighting those can be a big draw. Consider hosting a Create a Creature Contest, a Mystery Dinner, or a Little Coffee Shop of Horrors.

Teen Read Week is a great idea, but why not make it Teen Read Month? It is almost easier to stretch the time out a little rather than try to fit several programs or events in one week, especially if that week coincides with local homecomings and more. While a national theme is chosen each year, Teen Read Week is really a library's chance to celebrate teen reading in any way they choose. Fewer teens are reading for pleasure than ever, so it is imperative to highlight the joys of reading in some way at every library.

One simple Teen Read Week activity would be to a hide a special bookmark in the teen area each day and to give a small prize to the teen who finds it. Another easy celebration idea is to give teens candy or pens at the checkout or other service desks in the library. Displays could highlight the national theme, local reading initiatives, or favorite genres or authors each day or week during October. In addition, almost any of the programs in this book could be used to celebrate Teen Read Week.

Create a Creature Contest

A drawing contest is a great way to attract creative teens to the library. In addition, the entries can provide fabulous decoration for any part of the library. This will in turn attract the families of those involved to your library. A good theme for an art contest is "Create a Creature," timely for October but also appropriate for fantasy-themed reading programs.

PREPARATION TIME   4 hours, plus 2 more hours if awards reception is held

LENGTH OF PROGRAM   1 month

NUMBER OF TEENS   More than 50 entries would make judging difficult

SUGGESTED AGE RANGE   Grades 7–12

SHOPPING LIST   Poster board or other materials needed to mount entries
Prizes
Food: fruit and cookies for reception (optional)

SETUP   The preparation for this program involves technical considerations, target marketing, judging, and display development. The program could run for the entire month of October, with entries put up as they come in. But, given that many people procrastinate, the library could be left with a lot of blank space until right before Halloween. Judging art does not take as much time as judging writing, however, so entries could be turned in during the first two weeks in October, judging could be done in one weekend, and the creatures could displayed through Halloween, to make a timely display.

Technical considerations involve how the items will be displayed in the future. Work out scanning elements if the library will post winning creatures on its website or reproduce them on bookmarks, posters, and the like. Such decisions should be made before the program is publicized, as they may require that entries be created in a particular way, such as by using a fine-point black felt-tip marker.

Choose and reserve a display space in the library, and determine if all entries will need to be the same size and how they will be mounted. Again, this should be done before the program is advertised anywhere. A sample Create a Creature form that helped address issues of uniformity in style and size is included in the appendix.

It is possible to offer this contest for the entire range of teens from twelve to eighteen years of age, but because older high school students may have specialized art training, it may be desirable to have two divisions of competition: one for junior high schoolers and one for high schoolers. Entries could also be grouped by type of creature, especially when the contest is tied to a reading theme. For example, there could be separate categories of competition for dragons, multiheaded creatures, and humorous creatures with the best names. This approach allows for different types of winners and may be less intimidating to younger teens.

Invite local college art teachers or art store owners to be judges if previous art contests have attracted a lot of entries or interest. If this art contest is a new program, nonprofessional judges are OK. Using school teachers can be a problem as some of their students may be entered in the contest. Be sure to include some teens and library staff in the judging as well.

Two Weeks before Contest Starts

Again, fall programs have lots of competition. Luckily, this one lends itself to eye-catching displays in the library. Book displays, posters of creatures, and stuffed monsters all can catch the attention of possible contestants. Notices to art teachers should go out mid-September. Media centers should be supplied with entry forms and attractive signs as well, because students spend free time there—time that could be spent creating a creature! Also contact managers of local art supply stores about the contest. They may donate prizes or gift certificates.

Once a few entries are put up, more will follow, so be sure to contact any teens you personally know who are interested in art or fantasy and encourage them to enter early.

MAKE IT HAPPEN

Judging should be done over a short time period, such as a weekend. Each judge could write down and rank three to five favorites, depending on the number of entries and if there are categories. Average the judges' responses, and pin ribbons or other notices on the winners. Scan any creatures that will be made into bookmarks or displayed in other ways and put them back on display.

Winners and nonwinners should be notified as soon as possible after the ribbons have been awarded. The sample letter for nonwinners of the April Poetry Contest, included in the appendix, can be adapted for nonwinners of this contest. Winners could receive prizes such as gift certificates to local art stores or bookstores, art supplies, sketchbooks, or simply nice certificates from the library.

Consider honoring all entrants at a reception. Invite all artists and their families to attend, and serve fruit and cookies near the display. Though the winners will be especially delighted to see their ribbons, all of the teens who entered will feel appreciated at this type of event.

Mystery Dinner

Murder mystery programs are popular with both teens and adults. A teen program can use teen advisory board members as actors and the library as a setting to provide some humor for audience members. A dinner or meal setting gives pacing to the program and fills time between acts. While such a program can have elaborate costuming, rehearsed scenes, and sets, it does not have to.

The program begins, if possible, with a real-life detective discussing how he or she works to solve crimes. Then that detective interrogates the suspects (volunteer teen actors) for the audience. Working as a team, the teens at each table discuss the interrogations and decide which suspect is the murderer. The first table to solve the crime and bring their answer to the librarian wins.

PREPARATION TIME 4 hours, plus two 1-hour rehearsals

LENGTH OF PROGRAM 2½ hours

NUMBER OF TEENS 25–35 audience members plus 6 teen actors

SUGGESTED AGE RANGE Grades 7–12

SHOPPING LIST Food: pizza and beverages for audience and cast members
(the cast can eat when they arrive)

Ice cream bar supplies: ice cream, selection of sauces, cherries, cones or bowls, sprinkles, whipped cream, nuts, bananas, wafers, spoons

Paper plates, napkins

Prizes for winners: mystery books or small gift certificates to McDonald's or a favorite teen hangout

Token of appreciation for detective: book or similar item, for police officers cannot accept monetary gifts

Decorations: Ellison magnifying glasses and footprints leading up to the room add a festive air

Props: plastic evidence bags, letters, photo of person posing as a dead body

Pencils for audience members so they can make notes in their dossiers

SETUP

One Month before Program

It is not a good idea to advertise a murder in the library! Instead, make a bulletin board display with the question "Who Killed Anita V. Cation?" followed immediately by "Teen Mystery Program." Splatters of red paint will be effective in getting attention. You may want to require a fee of $5 for this program to ensure that registered teens will come and that you will have enough food.

Put bookmarks or flyers describing the program inside a display of mystery books for teens. Put Ellison footprints around the teen area leading up to the bulletin board or display. Put a tape outline of a body on the floor of the teen center, clearly near a display.

Recruit six teen volunteers to play the suspects in the mystery. Choose teens who you know can think on their feet, or add a few dynamic library staff members. You should also have some staff prepared to jump in if a suspect does not show up.

Suspects will be largely responsible for their own costumes. Make it clear that suspects need to dress in character and give them some direction if needed, but you will find that creative teens may enjoy inventing their own look for their character. For example, Alota Dinero may want to wear lots of glittering jewelry and a boa or fake furs. Ask suspects to come to one rehearsal in costume so you can take pictures for publicity.

Recruit a member of the local police force to give a short, program-opening talk and to interrogate the suspects.

Create a script outline for each suspect and the detective that briefly describes the crime and the suspects' characteristics and relationships. A script outline that may be adapted to your specific situation is presented in the appendix.

Two Weeks before Program

At a rehearsal, take photos of the suspects in costume and mount the photos on a bulletin board under the headline "WANTED for the Murder of Anita V. Cation." Include a full description of the program and how to register.

If you are using the script outline supplied in the appendix and adapting it for your library, be sure to schedule two rehearsals with the actors. Phone the teen you would like to be the killer ahead of time—in this script it is Ann Beans—and impress upon that person that secrecy is essential. At rehearsals, practice interviewing your suspects, helping them improvise their answers. Remember, they are given only bare facts. Your detective, which may be you or another strong actor in the absence of police help, should be tough. Teens should be ready to act defensive and insolent in the face of brutal questioning. If a member of the local police department will be playing the detective, she should be given her version of the script outline early enough to familiarize herself with her role and ask any questions she may have, but she will not be expected to attend rehearsals.

The teen suspects will have no idea of what the detective may ask, which will lend credibility to the program. Rehearsals can focus on basic questions, covering the wheres and hows of the facts provided in the script outline. If pre-scripted questions and answers were used, the results would be stiff and obvious. This version is more like a real investigation. If necessary, on the night of the program, ask suspects to arrive early enough to run through questioning again. Also ask the detective to insert a brief pause after each interrogation to allow audience members time to make a few notes.

If you are going to have simple props, such as items of evidence in plastic bags or a photo of someone posing as a dead body, be sure to allow yourself a few hours to prepare those, or to have the teens do so.

Day of Program   Set up tables with four to six chairs each for the audience. It is advisable to ask for a nominal fee for this program to ensure that the registered teens will attend and will eat the food ordered. Arrange tables along the wall with pizza, paper plates, cups, napkins, and drinks for teens to serve themselves.

Each table of teens will compete as a team. Set a Mystery Dinner Dossier for each teen on the tables along with one answer sheet and pencils for taking notes. (A sample Mystery Dinner Dossier is included in the appendix.) A table with two microphones should be at the front of the room, visible to all audience members. Place six chairs off to the side for suspects who are waiting to be questioned. Decorations do not need to be elaborate for this program. Die-cut shapes of magnifying glasses or footprints scattered on the audience tables add to the ambience but are not necessary.

While the detective questions the suspects, staff will quietly set up the ice cream bar. The pizza could be cleared away and the same table used. The line for the ice cream bar will move faster if some bowls of ice cream are already on the table so that teens can simply pick one up and add the toppings that are set out. It is a good idea to have a staff member or two on hand to help with aerosol whipped cream and to keep filling bowls with ice cream.

MAKE IT HAPPEN   If there are some teens who want to be involved but do not want to act in front of their peers, consider making them hosts for the evening, or ask staff to take on this role. Hosts should greet audience members and check them in if they are registered. Then they should invite guests to take some pizza and choose a table to sit at. They should also encourage guests to prepare for the evening by reading the Mystery Dinner Dossier while they wait for the program to begin. Audience members who arrive alone should be invited to join a team by sitting at one of the tables and should also be shown where to find the pizza and drinks. Here is a possible timeline for the event:

6:00 P.M.	Suspects arrive and have some time to review their questioning
6:30 P.M.	Audience members arrive and are invited to eat
6:50 P.M.	Host reviews the timeline for the evening and introduces the detective, who may make some brief opening remarks
6:55–7:40 P.M.	Questioning of suspects
7:30 P.M.	Staff sets up ice cream bar
7:45–8:10 P.M.	Ice cream bar open; teams deliberate while suspects individually travel from table to table to allow guests further questions
8:20 P.M.	All teams must turn in their answer sheets
8:25 P.M.	Killer is revealed and prizes are awarded to the winning team

As soon as a team thinks they know the solution to the mystery, they should write both the killer's name and why he or she committed the crime on their answer sheet and give the sheet to the host. On each answer sheet the host will record the team members' names and the time the sheet was turned in. The first table to solve the crime and bring their answer to the host wins. The winners should not be announced, however, until the murderer has been dramatically revealed.

Once all the answers have been collected, assemble all the suspects, still in costume. Read the first solution and ask the suspect it names if he or she committed the crime. The suspects must respond in character but should feel free to bluff. Continue reading the solutions and accusing the suspects until, ultimately, the killer admits his or her guilt and is led away by the detective.

After the murderer is revealed, it is time to announce the winning team. Prizes may include mystery books or candy bars. Consider offering an additional prize for the most creative answer. Teams can come up with very elaborate reasons for the murder, even if they name the wrong killer, so a creativity prize gives teens a chance to win something that does not depend on speed.

Little Coffee Shop of Horrors

Themed coffeehouse programs are great for Halloween or Teen Read Week. Having a horror theme adds some different sorts of creative activities to a typical evening of poetry reading.

PREPARATION TIME	1 hour
LENGTH OF PROGRAM	1½–2 hours
NUMBER OF TEENS	No limit, but it is a good idea to take sign-ups at the door for all who want to perform, to ensure that everyone has a chance
SUGGESTED AGE RANGE	Grades 7–12
SHOPPING LIST	Food: Halloween-related snacks, such as candy corn and pumpkins; cookies, chips, pretzels; Hawaiian punch and plastic eyeballs to float in it
	Scary decorations, including black tablecloths, cobwebs, and glow-in-the-dark skeletons
	Prizes for drawings

SETUP   If you presented the September Scary Story Contest described in this book, consider inviting the winners to read at this event. You could issue the invitations either when you notify teens that they have won or through subsequent communication. Some writers are shy, so it may not be a good idea to require that winners read. Ask all who are interested in reading their winning stories to register with staff before the event. Then schedule enough time for the stories to be read at either the beginning or the end of the program.

One Week before Program   Choose some backup activities from the suggestions under "Make It Happen" in the event that teens are shy about performing and ice breakers are needed. Check if the library has the supplies needed for the activities you select and, if not, add them to your shopping list for the event.

Day of Program   While decorations are fun, too many can make the event unappealing to older teens. Put out some dark and dreary decorations, such as black tablecloths with cobwebs. To maintain the coffeehouse atmosphere, plan on keeping the lights low except over the performer.

Put a bowl or two of snacks at each table, and set up the punch table at the back of the room.

Provide a box or cauldron where teens can deposit raffle slips for periodic drawings for prizes. If you have a shy group, consider having small novelty prizes for anyone who performs.

Pull together a display of scary books and poetry that people can read instead of their own creative work. Some teens may want to check out these titles on the way out.

MAKE IT HAPPEN   Start the event by letting any teens who want to perform do so. If the group is shy, here are a few suggestions for ice-breaking activities:

Mask-Making or Face-Painting Station. Get some simple Halloween makeup or mask-making supplies and sample pictures, and encourage teens to be creative.

Ghost (Bingo) Game. Print out bingo cards with the word GHOST replacing the usual BINGO heading and play the game.

Scariest Poem. Ask audience members to suggest ten scary words, and write their choices where everyone can see them. Then ask teens to write a poem using as many of the words as possible. After a few minutes, ask volunteers to read their poems and then select the scariest poem by having audience members applaud for their favorites. A variation would be to have a contest for scariest rhyming poem.

Scary Lit. Read parts of famous scary poems or descriptions of famous monsters and see if teens can identify them.

Create a Story. Read the phrase "She walked down the creaky stairs and saw . . ." and invite tablemates to take turns adding to the phrase until they have created an entire story.

Look into the Future. Set up a Ouija board, a Magic 8 Ball, and tarot cards and let teens try them out. Providing related instruction sheets and books will add to the fun. A similar approach can be used with palm reading.

Holding periodic drawings throughout the evening will motivate teens to stay for the entire program and encourage attendance by teens who may not want to perform in front of others. Prizes can be simple, such as candy bars or horror books.

OCTOBER PASSIVE PROGRAMS

Famous Monsters. Create a sheet that presents a list of famous monsters, such as Big Foot, the Loch Ness Monster, and Dracula, and a list of the monsters' descriptions. Then ask teens to match the name of each monster to its description.

Make a Difference. Create a sheet that lists the names of charitable and socially conscious organizations on one side and causes on the other side. Ask teens to match each agency to its cause. Spotlight local or national groups, and provide website addresses and other information so that teens can learn more about them.

OCTOBER RESOURCES

Teen Read Week

Alessio, Amy, and Kevin Scanlon. *Teen Read Week: A Manual for Participation*. Chicago: YALSA, 2002.

Young Adult Library Services Association. The Official Teen Read Week Website (loaded with booklists and ideas for each year's theme). http://www.ala.org/ala/yalsa/teenreading/trw/teenreadweek.htm.

Create a Creature

Ames, Lee J. *Draw Fifty Beasties and Yugglies and Turnover Uglies*. New York: Doubleday, 1988.

———. *Draw Fifty Monsters, Creeps, Superheroes, Demons, Dragons, Nerds*. New York: Doubleday, 1983.

Bolognese, Don. *The Way to Draw and Color Monsters*. New York: Random House, 1991.

Hart, Christopher. *Anime Mania: How to Draw Characters for Japanese Animation*. New York: Watson-Guptill, 2002.

McLaughlin, Frank. *How to Draw Monsters: For Comics*. Oakland, CA: Renaissance Books, 2001.

Sullivan, Howard. *How to Draw Digimon Monsters*. New York: Scholastic, 2000.

Display Ideas
Toy monsters, superheroes, cobwebs, skeletons; also graphic novels with superhero themes, such as those featuring Spiderman, Batman, Captain America, and the Incredible Hulk

Mystery Madness

Display Ideas
Footprints on floor leading
to display, magnifying
glasses, pieces from
a Clue game

A few of the great mystery and suspense authors for teens are

J. B. Cheany	Gail Giles
Agatha Christie	Graham McNamee
Caroline Cooney	Joan Lowery Nixon
Gillian Cross	Carol Plum-Ucci
Lois Duncan	Vivian Vande Velde

November

November, with lots of school projects due before Thanksgiving and the fast approach of the holidays, may not be the best month for teen programming. But teens need stress relief like anyone else, and honoring Veterans Day at the beginning of the month is important too. While teens may not be interested in all the dates and details of wars in history, some may enter the armed forces directly after high school. It is possible to bring history to life with reenactors, as in the Underground Railroad program described in the February chapter, or to celebrate with the Origami Patriotic Peace Project.

Thanksgiving turns thoughts to food. See if your library could clear fines for teens and other patrons who bring in canned goods and other nonperishables for local food pantries during this month. Some fun food programs for teens can be offered too, such as Eat It Up and the Pizza-Tasting Party.

Origami Patriotic Peace Project

November, in conjunction with Veterans Day, is a good time for a project promoting peace, though of course there is no bad time for that kind of initiative. The folding of a thousand cranes is a tradition made famous by the story of Sadako, a young girl who became ill as a result of the radiation at Hiroshima. She wanted to fold a thousand cranes, because according to an old legend she would become well if she completed them. Her classmates raised money for a monument in her memory. Paper cranes have thus become a symbol of peace. (See resources at the end of this chapter to learn all the details of Sadako's story.) This program involves teens in folding cranes and then stringing them for display in the library or elsewhere.

Folding a thousand cranes is an enormous undertaking, so this is a good opportunity to reach out to teens in schools, teen centers, churches, scout troops, and throughout your community. If the project continues over four to five months, a thousand cranes should be ready to display for a Veterans Day memorial.

PREPARATION TIME 15 hours

LENGTH OF PROGRAM A series of 1-hour folding events spread over 4–5 months, ending on Veterans Day

NUMBER OF TEENS 20 teens maximum per folding session

SUGGESTED AGE RANGE Grade 5 through adults

SHOPPING LIST Red, white, and blue origami paper (regular paper can work, but you will want light, small cranes on the strings)

20 skeins of red, white, blue, or just white embroidery floss for stringing

Darning needles with large eyes

Bars or hangers on which to tie the strings to so they will not get tangled

SETUP Spending enough time to make and string the cranes while keeping the momentum going is crucial for this program. It may be a good idea to have an origami program in the summer and to keep the teens folding at school and youth group events throughout the fall. Stringing the cranes as they are collected is essential. If the initial origami program is held at the library in July, cranes could be collected through mid-October so they may go on display for Veterans Day. If enough are folded, or if there is a great deal of interest in this type of program, some cranes could be displayed for a September 11 memorial.

Order paper and gather materials on how to fold cranes at least a month before attempting to present this program for the first time. This will enable you to learn both how to fold cranes and how to make a display. Learning how to fold cranes is the hardest part of this program. Host folding and stringing parties or events at the library. Teach a core group of teens how to do it, then have them teach others. This is a good drop-in event on days off from school, or could be a program in itself when accompanied by a video demonstration, a reading of the story of Sadako, and some stringing. Invite teens to write the name of a veteran or someone killed on September 11 either outside or inside each folded crane. This truly makes the culminating event a memorial.

When preparing for a folding event, arrange tables in a U shape so that teens can easily see the instructor or any audiovisual equipment that will be used. Staff will still have to go to each table to watch progress. Folding paper and simple instructions should be placed on each table. If there are many teens who are new to folding cranes, put out squares of scratch paper for them to practice on. When they have mastered the practice cranes, they can move on to the red, white, and blue paper for the display. Refreshments such as cookies are a good way to reward folders, but to keep the cranes clean, save any treats until folding has been completed.

Decorate drop boxes in red, white, and blue and distribute them to community agencies and school media centers along with a large stack of instruction sheets on folding cranes and an explanation of the program. Offer to present a folding demonstration at the schools and teen agencies. Hanging some finished cranes at each place will help keep the program on everyone's mind. Just keep track of how many cranes you leave in each place so that you can retrieve them in time for the memorial.

Seeing a few hanging cranes helps people imagine what the total effect will be when all thousand cranes are strung up. Invite teens to decide where the cranes will ultimately hang. The display will take up a surprisingly large amount of space, especially since the cranes need enough room to fly without getting tangled. Amy Alessio had the cranes hang at the local arts center as one part of a September 11 memorial, and others were sent to the American Airlines headquarters. After the cranes were taken down from the arts center, some were sent to an organization that collects cranes for use in future memorials.

To string folded cranes, thread a six-foot strand of embroidery floss through the eye of a darning needle. Knot one end several times to form a sizable knot. Pierce a crane vertically from its stomach to its back and gently slide the bird down the string until it sits on top of the knot. The knot should not be pulled through any layer of paper in the crane! Leave at least six inches of string and make another sizable knot. Thread another crane down the string, leave another six inches of string, and make another knot. Continue in this way until you have ten to fourteen cranes per string.

MAKE IT HAPPEN   To create context, during the first folding session at the library, introduce the story of Sadako and the thousand paper cranes. Show a video about how to fold cranes, demonstrate the process yourself, or have teen instructors do the teaching. Have everyone practice folding regular paper until they are ready to use the more expensive origami paper. Circulate from table to table to provide individual help. This event should garner fifty to one hundred cranes. Provide a sign-up sheet so that interested participants can volunteer to fold more cranes at home. Include lines for name, contact information, and number of cranes promised. Then make sure that each volunteer receives the appropriate amount of origami paper. Some will not return either cranes or unused paper, and mistakes will be made, but having volunteers sign up increases motivation. You may want to offer some incentives for teens who fold large numbers of cranes, such as autographed books or origami craft kits.

Have knotted string available at all times so that loose cranes can be strung as they come in. Amy Alessio even received cranes via the library drive-through, and often in large amounts. Tie a couple of strings at a time on a hanger or from a hanging bar, allowing plenty of space between them. Hanging some partially completed strings in a visible place in the library will keep the momentum going.

September
Explain the program and hold mini folding demonstrations at teen centers, after-school activities, the YMCA, park district teen events, and the like. This will promote the library and the program at the same time! It is also a good way to get out and see what the other centers are doing for teens. Encourage each center to commit to folding at least one hundred cranes, or have a little competition among the different teen centers with the promise of pizza or some other prize for the group that produces the most cranes. Be sure to include your library teens in the competition.

By mid-September, you will get an idea of how the project is going. If it looks as if you might not have enough cranes, step up your promotion of the program. If you think you may have too many cranes, see if local city officials would like to display some for a September 11 memorial.

October
Start putting garbage or dry cleaning bags over the hangers with completed strings of cranes and transporting them to the designated display site.

November
At the display site, hang a poster explaining the program, and make sure that the cranes are all in place by Veterans Day. Many official places will be closed on that day, so you may need to unveil the display a day earlier or later. Be sure to take pictures of the hanging cranes and use some to create a flyer for the public to pick up at the library.

December through February
Write thank-yous to agencies that folded a large number of cranes and award any prizes you may have promised them. Invite your teens to help decide where the cranes will go after the display is over. For example, you could donate them to agencies that collect cranes or send them to Japan. Or it may be nice to hang a few as souvenirs in each agency that worked on them.

Eat It Up

This program, which features simple recipes that are healthy and fun to make, is a great way to introduce teens to the kitchen. It can also be used as an addition to a life skills program for graduating high school seniors. The best way to a teen's heart is through the stomach, so during the program, while their mouths are full and their stomachs are happy, take the opportunity to recommend books for teens on cooking and simple meals they can make for themselves. You might also talk up some going-to-college/on-your-own/get-your-act-together books. There are some listed in the November resources.

PREPARATION TIME 1 hour plus shopping time

LENGTH OF PROGRAM 2 hours

NUMBER OF TEENS 25

SUGGESTED AGE RANGE 11–18 years

SHOPPING LIST See the recipes in the "Make It Happen" section. Depending on the number of participants, you may need to adjust the quantities to ensure that everyone gets to sample each dish.

SETUP

Day before Program Go through each recipe that you want to demonstrate and prepare the ingredients in advance. For example, do any chopping that needs to be done and refrigerate all perishables. It is important to be near appliances for almost all the recipes. Check the demonstration area to make sure you have all the necessary appliances, utensils, and other equipment.

Day of Program Set up a demonstration table near the cooking area so that teens can see what you are doing. The table should be large enough to accommodate you and one or more teen helpers.

In a separate area for eating, set up several tables, each with six chairs. Cover the tables with paper tablecloths. If you can, find clip art of college kids, cooking utensils, food, kitchen appliances, and so forth. Arrange these on the tablecloths to make your setup interesting.

One Hour before Program Group the ingredients, utensils, and equipment you will need for each recipe in stations or sections near the demonstration area. Review the sequence of ingredients and tasks to ensure that your setup will enable you to move smoothly through your presentation.

MAKE IT HAPPEN Demonstrate each recipe with the help of a few teen volunteers from the audience. To broaden participation, use different volunteers for each recipe. You may serve each item as it is cooked or hold a sit-down tasting after all cooking is completed. In either case, serve portions that are small enough for each teen to sample each dish.

Before the cooking begins, briefly discuss the basics of kitchen safety. As you start each recipe, review any advance preparation, such as chopping, that has already been done. Then proceed through the recipe, explaining each step as you demonstrate.

Variation   Group teens into five- or six-member teams, with each team working on a different recipe. If space and equipment are limited, have one group cook and demonstrate while the others watch and sample some of the previously cooked results. Read each step of the recipe aloud as the teens are demonstrating. As each item is cooked, serve it in small amounts so that all teens can sample it.

Recipes
Veggie Quesadillas

8 burrito-size tortillas

2 cups shredded mozzarella cheese

1 2-ounce can sliced black olives

1 cup diced red bell peppers, green bell peppers
   and green onions, mixed

Hot pepper sauce

Salsa

> Heat a large frying pan or griddle over medium heat.
>
> Place one tortilla flat on the frying pan.
>
> After 1 minute flip the tortilla over.
>
> Sprinkle a little more than ¼ cup cheese on the tortilla, followed by the olives, pepper mixture, and a sprinkle of hot sauce.
>
> Place another tortilla on top to make a sandwich.
>
> Cover the frying pan with a lid.
>
> After 1 minute, flip the quesadilla.
>
> When the cheese has melted on the inside, remove the quesadilla.
>
> Repeat with remaining ingredients.
>
> Cut the quesadilla into triangles and serve with salsa on the side.

Bean Quesadillas

2 burrito-size tortillas

½ cup refried beans

¼ cup diced red bell pepper

¼ cup each shredded mozzarella and red cheddar,
   or ½ cup shredded Mexican cheese blend

1 tomato

1 container of sour cream

Olive oil

Salsa

> Heat an electric skillet to 325 degrees.
>
> Brush one side of each tortilla with olive oil.
>
> Place one tortilla oil side down on the heated skillet.

Evenly spread the refried beans, cheese, and salsa on the tortilla.

Top with the second tortilla.

Cook at 325 degrees for 5 minutes.

To serve, cut into wedges and garnish with tomatoes and sour cream.

Mexicali Popcorn

1/3 cup butter

1 tablespoon dry taco seasoning mix

1 tablespoon dry chopped chives

4 quarts popped popcorn

In small saucepan, melt butter over low heat.

Add taco seasoning and chives.

Blend.

Pour over popcorn in large serving bowl and toss lightly.

Serve at once.

Chocolate Peanut Butter Pizza

1/2 cup butter

1/2 cup sugar

1/2 cup firmly packed brown sugar

1/2 cup peanut butter

1 egg

1 cup all-purpose flour

1 teaspoon baking soda

1 12-ounce package semi-sweet chocolate chips, divided

1/4 cup peanut butter

toppings:

Heath candy bars, coarsely chopped
Butterfinger candy bars, coarsely chopped
Miniature marshmallows
Maraschino cherries
Chopped nuts (hazelnuts, peanuts, almonds, pecans)
Shredded sweetened coconut
Banana, peeled and sliced
Melted white chocolate
Dried apricots, chopped
Dried cherries

Preheat oven to 350 degrees.

Lightly grease a 12- to 14-inch pizza pan.

In a large bowl, cream butter, sugar, brown sugar, and peanut butter until light and fluffy. Beat in egg, flour, and baking soda.

Stir in half of the chocolate chips.

Using your fingers, spread or press the dough onto the pizza pan, leaving a 1-inch space around the edge to allow the cookie to spread as it bakes.

Bake 18 to 24 minutes, until light brown.

Remove from oven and immediately sprinkle remaining chocolate chips and drop spoonfuls of peanut butter over the top.

Let pizza rest for 5 minutes, or until chocolate is shiny and soft.

Add toppings of your choice.

Let pizza cool before cutting and serving.

Orange Julius

1 6-ounce can frozen orange juice

1 cup milk

1 cup water

¼ cup sugar (or less, to taste)

1 teaspoon vanilla

5–6 ice cubes

Place all ingredients in blender. Blend about 30 seconds. Serve.

Helpful Hints

Always put safety, knowledge, and use of proper procedures first.

For added expertise, invite a local home sciences educator or county extension agent to do a presentation on cooking, nutrition, home safety, or other related topics.

Have teens choose favorite recipes to cut out and glue into their own mini cookbooks to take home. Make and decorate covers out of cardboard, card stock, recycled file folders, or some other heavy paper.

Be sure to make photocopies of the recipes to hand out to participants. Include the reading lists with the recipes.

Pizza-Tasting Party

Who doesn't like pizza? Attract busy teens to the library and feature local restaurants with a pizza-tasting contest.

PREPARATION TIME	4 hours
LENGTH OF PROGRAM	2 hours
NUMBER OF TEENS	25
SUGGESTED AGE RANGE	Grades 6–12
SHOPPING LIST	Assorted kinds of soda, lemonade (for those who do not drink soda) Paper napkins and plates

SETUP

Two Weeks before Program

Solicit donations by calling the managers of local pizza places and explaining that you are planning a pizza-tasting party for teens at the library. Tell them that participants will rate the pizzas and that the results will be announced. Agree in advance on the number and kinds of pizza each donor will supply. Be sure to have a good variety that will accommodate teens' various tastes and diets. Try to interest some small local media as well. Media coverage makes the event pay off for everyone and gives local businesses opportunity for free advertising.

One Week before Program

Recruit drivers to pick up the pizzas on the day of the program. Make sure that all the participating pizzerias are covered and that drivers know where and when to pick up their assigned pizzas. Schedule the pickups to ensure that the pizzas will arrive in plenty of time for the party.

Develop a simple rating sheet for the pizzas. List the restaurants and the types of pizza they provided. Teens can just circle the one they liked best. If desired, you could ask teens to pick their favorite by flavor category, such as cheese, sausage, the works.

Also include a section for comments, which are likely to be hysterically funny.

Three Days before Program

Call the managers of the pizzerias to confirm that they still intend to participate and to double-check the quantity, size, and kinds of pizza they plan to send. Tell them the time at which you will send someone to pick up the pizza on the day of the program. If any of the pizzerias drop out, be prepared to make alternative plans for obtaining an adequate supply of pizzas.

Two to Three Hours before Program

Make one final call to the restaurant managers to confirm that they intend to have the promised pizzas ready for pickup at the designated time.

One Hour before Program	Set up several tables just for the pizzas. Make a label for each pizza that identifies its ingredients and the name of the restaurant that provided it. Cut each pizza into pieces that are half the usual size. Leave paper plates and napkins at one end of each pizza table.

Provide a separate table for beverages. Of course, soda is the perfect companion to pizza. Also keep on hand water and lemonade for those who do not drink soda.

Set up tables with four to six chairs each at which teens can enjoy their pizza. Place rating forms and pencils on each table.

MAKE IT HAPPEN As teens arrive, they can chat with their friends, mingle, and listen to music. When all teens have arrived, invite them to start begin sampling pizza. They can start at any pizza and work their way across the tables. If twenty-five teens are registered, make sure there are at least twenty-five pieces of each kind of pizza. Cut small pieces if you have to. Encourage teens to pace themselves so they do not become sick!

When all teens have tasted the pizzas, collect the rating forms and tally the votes. While the teens are waiting for the results, they can listen to music or even some quick book talks from staff. When the ratings are tallied, announce the top three favorites.

To add to the festivities, consider having a drawing for a gift certificate from one of the pizza restaurants.

NOVEMBER PASSIVE PROGRAMS

Native American Match-Up. Create a sheet that presents a list of tribal names and a labeled map of reservations. Matching each tribe to its current reservation will help teens realize how few reservations are left and if there is one close by.

Famous Native Americans. Create a sheet that lists the names of famous Native Americans, from Squanto to modern-day politicians and actors, in one column and the reasons for their fame in a second column. Ask teens to match each person to his or her claim to fame.

Pizza Topping Chart. On a bulletin board, make a large grid listing every possible pizza topping, from pepperoni to vegetables to anchovies, and including a few exotic items such as pineapple. Invite teens to put a checkmark next to their favorite topping and watch the progress of the voting.

NOVEMBER RESOURCES

Hiroshima and Crane Folding

Coerr, Eleanor. *Sadako and the Thousand Cranes*. New York: Putnam, 1977.

Grant, R. G. *Hiroshima and Nagasaki*. Austin, TX: Raintree Steck-Vaughn, 1998.

Hook, Jason. *Hiroshima, August 6, 1945*. Austin, TX: Raintree Steck-Vaughn, 2003.

How to Fold a Paper Crane. Video. Santa Cruz, CA: George Levenson, 1994.

Ishii, Takayuki. *One Thousand Paper Cranes: The Story of Sadako and the Children's Peace Statue*. New York: Dell Laurel-Leaf, 1997.

Lawton, Clive. *Hiroshima: The Story of the First Atom Bomb*. Cambridge, MA: Candlewick, 2004.

MacEachin, Douglas. *Final Months of the War with Japan*. Washington, DC: Central Intelligence Agency, Center for the Study of Intelligence, 1998.

Morin, John, and Jack Crane. *Ultimate Origami Kit: The Complete Step-by-Step Guide to the Art of Paper Folding*. Scranton, PA: Courage, 2000.

Sherrow, Victoria. *The Making of the Atom Bomb*. San Diego, CA: Lucent, 2000.

Tames, Richard. *Hiroshima: The Shadow of the Bomb*. Chicago: Heinemann Library, 2001.

Display Ideas

Paper cranes strung on threads and hung around the teen center, a chart tracking how many cranes have been folded so far toward the goal of one thousand, sheets of origami paper and handouts with instructions on how to fold cranes along with a box to collect them in; books on any war in addition to the origami titles for this program

Food, Cooking, and Independence

Bellenir, Karen. *Diet Information for Teens*. Detroit: Omnigraphics, 2001.

Carle, Megan, and Jill Carle. *Teens Cook*. Berkeley, CA: Ten Speed Press, 2004.

Columbia University's Health Education Program. *The "Go Ask Alice" Book of Answers: A Guide to Good Physical, Sexual, and Emotional Health*. New York: Henry Holt, 1998.

Flipse, Robyn. *Fighting the Freshman Fifteen: A College Woman's Guide to Getting Real about Food and Keeping the Pounds Off*. New York: Three Rivers Press, 2002.

Hanson, Jennifer. *The Real Freshman Handbook: A Totally Honest Guide to Life on Campus*. 2nd ed. Boston: Houghton Mifflin, 2002.

Mills, Nancy, and Kevin Mills. *Help! My Apartment Has a Dining Room Cookbook*. Boston: Houghton Mifflin, 1999.

Nimetz, Alexandra, Jason Stanley, and Emeline Starr. *The Healthy College Cookbook*. Pownal, VT: Storey, 1999.

Patterson, Jean, and Diane Campbell. *Cooking outside the Pizza Box*. New York: Barron's, 2004.

Display Ideas

Pots and pans, kitchen implements

Raab, Evelyn. *Clueless in the Kitchen: A Cookbook for Teens*. Buffalo, NY: Firefly, 1998.

Taylor, Sally. *On My Own*. Tecumseh, KS: Silly Goose Productions, 2002.

Pizza

Showing the movie *Mystic Pizza* with Julia Roberts may set the mood while you are waiting for pizzas to bake.

German, Donna. *The Best Pizza Is Made at Home*. Hayward, CA: Bristol, 2000.

Morowitz, Harold. *The Thermodynamics of Pizza*. New Brunswick, NJ: Rutgers University Press, 1992.

Scicolone, Charles and Michele. *Pizza*. New York: Broadway, 1999.

Watt, Fiona. *Pasta and Pizza for Beginners*. Tulsa, OK: Educational Development, 2003.

Display Ideas

Pizza baking stone, toy pizza parts, cutout paper pepperonis, mushrooms, and other ingredients to scatter on table

December

December brings rich holiday and cultural traditions. Introducing teens to a variety of customs can be fun as well as educational. Invite teens to share their heritage with others at the Tasting the World Food Fest. Show the diversity of holidays celebrated with a multicultural holiday crafts workshop.

Tasting the World Food Fest

There is no community in the United States today without cultural diversity. Having a program that highlights the different foods of the world is fun and educational for teens. Another possibility is to spotlight food from different states or regions of this country, which helps teens appreciate the rich traditions across our melting-pot land. Encourage members of your teen advisory board to learn about foods that are part of their ethnic tradition, or suggest that teens who want to go to college in a state far away learn about the foods from that area.

PREPARATION TIME	6 hours
LENGTH OF PROGRAM	1½–2 hours
NUMBER OF TEENS	40–50 maximum in audience
SUGGESTED AGE RANGE	Grades 6–9

SHOPPING LIST   The following list applies to any version of food sampling. More complex variations of the program may require additional food and supplies for cooking demonstrations.

> Paper plates
>
> Napkins
>
> Eating utensils
>
> Serving utensils
>
> Rubber gloves for servers
>
> Drinks, including ice or bottled water
>
> Cups
>
> Plastic tablecloths for audience tables

SETUP

One Month before Program

Research will take the most preparation time, followed by food prep, but this type of program can be done at varying levels of complexity. Teachers of foreign language or culture at local junior and senior highs may offer extra credit to students who help you, depending on the type of program you choose.

Try nontraditional methods of advertising this program, such as handing out fortune cookies with a flyer to promote an Asian or Chinese New Year cooking program.

If you will be doing any book talking, advertise the food fest by offering samples for teens to try. Display plenty of photos of foods around the library to send subliminal messages about the program.

Time and budget will dictate which version of this program can be attempted, but all are fun and educational as well as delicious. Provide lists of ingredients in all dishes served to guide teens with allergies.

Easy Programs   Find out if local high schools have culture or language clubs, such as a German Club. Invite club members to cohost a culturally authentic event, such as an Oktoberfest, with the library. The teens will have studied the foods and traditions, and you can help with the supplies.

Locate a variety of ethnic restaurants within your area and either ask for donations or purchase samples of typical foods. For example, purchase some pad thai from a Thai restaurant.

Hire a cook to demonstrate the preparation of ethnic foods, perhaps even sushi. There may be one or more staff members who make delicious ethnic treats for holidays every year and would be willing to demonstrate their preparations as well.

Moderately Demanding Programs   Invite TAB members to bring in foods that reflect their ethnic heritage. Favorite dishes made by their grandparents or another family member are particularly welcome. Plan on bringing plenty of food yourself in case some volunteers drop out. For example, Amy brings pizza or other hearty Italian food to go with her heritage.

Present a class in how to cook some basic ethnic dishes. (Note the easy cookbooks suggested in the December resources.) Featuring foods that are current fads increases the popularity of the program. For example, bubble tea was really popular in the Northwest a few years ago, and its popularity is spreading to the rest of the country. There are kits for making bubble tea that can be ordered online.

Elaborate Programs

Choose a country or a region of the United States and research its foods and traditions. The Mardi Gras celebration outlined in the February chapter is this sort of program. Your event could range from an elaborate discussion and tasting of historical Native American tribal dishes to a presentation and tasting of the types of hot dogs that are popular in various regions of the country. Examine, for example, what makes a Chicago hot dog distinctive. Or provide samples of a variety of coffees, teas, and hot chocolate, discuss their origins, and invite teens to comment on the differences in their tastes. Another possibility would be to create a program featuring foods from historical cookbooks

Holiday fare is always a popular theme for a tasting fest. Teens can learn about the traditions of eating black-eyed peas for the New Year, potato pancakes for Hanukkah, Swedish cookies for Christmas, and the like.

MAKE IT HAPPEN

To make whatever program you choose more fun and interactive, it is nice to have teens participate in the preparation. Teens should also leave with recipes for the foods that they sampled.

Taking registration for any type of food-related event is important to ensure that there is enough food for everyone. To avoid shortages if teens will be sampling foods from ethnic restaurants, for example, each person could receive tickets at the door to be turned in for one sample at each station. Set up tables with four to six chairs each at which people can eat and drink.

For a food demonstration, arrange chairs at tables so all teens can easily see the presentation. Consider covering the tables with plastic tablecloths so teens can prepare food at their own tables as they watch the demonstration. To ensure that all can hear the instructions, provide a microphone for the speaker. Recruiting enough help so that some people can circulate while others serve food will keep the program moving smoothly.

Send thank-you notes to any restaurants, cooks, teachers, and students who helped with the program. If the program was very popular, invite them to participate in the event again next year.

Holiday Crafts from Near and Far

December is a good time to talk about diversity in holiday celebrations without getting too involved in questions of religion. The activities suggested below are just a few options for a program that features a variety of holiday traditions. Other cultural practices, especially if they are specific to your community, could easily be substituted. A discussion of interesting holiday practices around the world can generate a lot of interest in other cultures. Take the opportunity to book talk holiday books.

PREPARATION TIME   1 hour plus shopping

LENGTH OF PROGRAM   2 hours

NUMBER OF TEENS   30

SUGGESTED AGE RANGE   12–18 years

SHOPPING LIST

Gift Wrap

Large rolls of colored paper (green, red, blue, yellow, and black) that will be precut into 36-inch-by-36-inch squares
Rubber bands
Tempera paint in assorted colors
Plastic bowls
Sponges in different shapes, sizes, and themes
Markers

Holiday Candy Wreaths

Paper plates	Assorted wrapped candy
Glue	Ribbon
Candy canes	Scissors

Holiday Cookie Decoration

Ready-made frosting	Assorted toppings
Plain sugar cookies	Paper plates
Sprinkles	

Kwanzaa Scarves

Two yards each of red, green, and black 54-inch- or 60-inch-wide polar fleece fabric cut into 2-inch strips

British Crackers

Cardboard tubes: old toilet paper or paper towel rolls (cut in half) are fine
Different types of wrapping paper: enough to cover 30 tubes and to allow 2 additional inches at each end of each tube
Curling ribbon or yarn: enough for two 12-inch pieces per teen
One hundred pieces of loose candy
Confetti or shredded paper: enough to give each teen about 1 tablespoon

SETUP	Gather as many different religious and secular symbols of winter holidays as you can find to use as decorations at the event. Include, for example, menorahs for Hanukkah, candles or kente cloth for Kwanzaa, and trees for Christmas.
One Week before Program	

Day of Program	Set up several tables with six to eight chairs per table. Cover each table with a paper tablecloth. Group the supplies for each activity and put each set of supplies in a separate place.

The cookies teens decorate can serve as refreshments. Supply hot cider, eggnog, hot chocolate, or other winter drinks.

MAKE IT HAPPEN	Let each teen choose a precut square of paper. On each table, place several bowls containing different colors of tempera paint and scatter sponges. Allow teens to decorate the paper anyway they would like, whether they prefer sponge painting, drawing, or some other technique. When they are finished, set the paper off to the side in order to dry. After thirty minutes to an hour, the paper should be ready to roll up, rubber-band, and take home to wrap presents with.
Gift Wrap	

Holiday Candy Wreaths	Give each teen a paper plate. Have them cut around the inside circle, and throw the inner one away. They will now have a donut-shaped paper plate. They can then arrange the candy into any shape they would like, and glue it onto the plate accordingly. Tie ribbon in a bow shape, and glue that onto the top of the plate. Set aside the wreathes to dry. When they are completely dry, and ready teens may take them home, or use them to decorate the teen area.

Holiday Cookie Decoration	Ask local schools or bakeries to provide plain sugar cookies in varying holiday shapes. This one is pretty straightforward. Give each teen a paper plate, and a few cookies. Spread the decoration supplies on each table, and allow them to decorate cookies any way they would like. Teens can consume their creations immediately, or wait until later.

Kwanzaa Scarves	Invite teens to braid three strips of polar fleece in the Kwanzaa colors. They can knot each end to make a simple scarf.

British Crackers	Explain to teens the tradition of Boxing Day in the British Isles. Then show them how to make crackers by rolling wrapping paper around cardboard tubes. Teens can tie curling ribbon or yarn around one end, put confetti and a few pieces of candy inside, and tie the other end. They may play by pulling on the ends with a friend until the cracker opens.

DECEMBER PASSIVE PROGRAMS

Holiday Traditions. On a bulletin board, put numbered photos or drawings depicting traditions and symbols for a wide variety of winter holidays, such as a Kinarah for Kwanzaa. Supply a list of holidays and ask teens to match each item on the bulletin board with the appropriate holiday.

Food for Thought. Enlarge a world map and put it on a bulletin board. Take pictures of traditional ethnic foods, laminate them, and affix double-sided tape or Velcro to the backs. Encourage teens to have fun trying to place each food on its country of origin. A similar activity can be presented on paper by creating a form that lists foods in one column and countries of origin in another for teens to match up.

DECEMBER RESOURCES

World of Cooking

Lerner Publications has a wonderful series called the Easy Menu Ethnic Cookbooks. These include *Cooking the German Way, . . . the Korean Way, . . . the Thai Way, . . . the Greek Way, . . . the Indian Way*, and many more. Blue Earth Books has a series on historical American cuisine called Exploring History through Simple Recipes that includes *Civil War Cooking, Oregon Trail Cooking*, and more.

Display Ideas

Pots and pans, cooking implements, spice jars, chopsticks, pictures of ethnic foods, flags from other countries

Holiday Traditions

Teen titles on holidays are limited, but general holiday craft and cooking books or children's holiday picture books may capture teens' fancy. Include traditions from many cultures, such as Ramadan, Kwanzaa, and Hanukkah.

Display Ideas

Menorah, Nativity scene, Christmas tree, dreidel, Kinarah, and other items from holidays during December

Conrad, Heather. *Lights of Winter*. Berkeley, CA: Lightport, 2001.

Luenn, Nancy. *Celebrations of Light: A Year of Holidays around the World*. New York: Atheneum, 1998.

Appendix

TEEN PROGRAM SURVEY

Please circle which of the following events you and your friends would attend at the library.

        A. Coffeehouse/Open Mike Night

        B. Teen Advisory Board

        C. Scrapbooking Workshop

        D. Band Night

What other types of programs would interest you?

_____

_____

_____

_____

_____

Please circle the days and times that are most convenient for you to attend programs.

A.	Monday	afternoon	evening
B.	Tuesday	afternoon	evening
C.	Wednesday	afternoon	evening
D.	Thursday	afternoon	evening
E.	Friday	afternoon	evening
F.	Saturday	afternoon	evening
G.	Sunday	afternoon	evening

National Library Week Teen Magazine Madness

Teens in grades 6 – 12 may enter drawings for Orlando Bloom posters or fast food gift certificates by filling out this survey. Please turn it in to the Reader Services Desk of the Central Library or at the branch libraries to enter.

Name: _____

Grade:_____

Phone:_____

Email: _____

1. How many magazines do you read at the library?

_____None

_____1 - 5 a week

_____1 - 5 a month

_____More than 5 a week

2. Do you prefer to read them at the library or to check them out?

_____At the library

_____Check them out

_____I'd like to check them out, but my favorites are usually not available

3. Please list at least 3 magazines that you like to read: _____
_____
_____

4. Which of these topics interest you? (Circle all that apply)

Music	Entertainment/Hollywood Stars
Creative Writing	Anime/Manga
Beauty/Fashion	Current Events
Cars	Video Games
College Life	Christian Life

Sports - please list _____

Ethnic interests - please list which ethnicities _____

Hobbies - please list _____

Other _____

5. If you could get magazines in another language, which language would you prefer? _____

6. What would you like to know about opportunities for your future? (Circle all that apply)

Job Opportunities	College Life
Types of Colleges	Travel Information
Other _____	

SCHAUMBURG TOWNSHIP DISTRICT LIBRARY

Central Library
130 South Roselle Road
Schaumburg, IL 60193
(847) 985-4000
Homepage: http://www.stdl.org

Hanover Park Branch Library
1570 Irving Park Road
Hanover Park, IL 60133
(630) 372-7800

Hoffman Estates Branch Library
1550 Hassell Road
Hoffman Estates, IL 60195
(847) 885-3511

TEEN
h a p p e n i n g s

Slay a Book

2005 TEEN SUMMER READING EVENT
MAY 16 - AUGUST 30

Slay a Book this summer and join in some spine-tingling events for teens. Designed by the Teen Advisory Board, programs will include Terror Tuesdays with scary movies, a Scary Scavenger Hunt and much more! Teens going into grades 7-12 can participate in the reading program by picking up a SCARE (BINGO-type) card from the Reader Services Desk at the central library or at the Hoffman Estates or Hanover Park branch libraries. Filling out review slips for books read will also enter teens into weekly prize drawings beginning in June. Finish the activities and/or books in a row of five squares to complete your SCARE card and pick up a prize between July 11-August 31. Prizes will include Schaumburg Flyers game vouchers and more. Ticket vouchers will be for the following Schaumburg Flyers game dates: July 21, July 25 or August 3. Game vouchers will be given for completing a row of BINGO while supplies last, but everyone who finishes the program will receive a prize!

Teen Invasion 2005

JUNE 13 - AUGUST 13

This award winning program for teens returns this summer to Schaumburg Township. Many more activities have been added to the program. Teens in grades 7-12 can earn tickets this summer by going to museums or theaters, reading, taking a class, registering bicycles with the police department, volunteering and more. Each activity earns teens tickets for drawings. Tickets can be turned in to the Reader Services Desk at the central library or the Hoffman Estates or Hanover Park branch libraries. Other participating agencies may collect tickets as well. Drawings will be held July 1, July 15, July 29, August 12. Prizes will include $50 and $25 gift certificates to area stores, free passes for local games, movie tickets and more!

Sisterhood of the Traveling Pants Event

TUESDAY, JUNE 14 / 2-4 P.M.
YOUTH SERVICES CRAFT ROOM

Did you read the wonderful Sisterhood books by Ann Brashares? Come experience the fun of sisterhood with this event. Teens in grades 7-12 will make jean purses,

friendship bracelets and more. Local artist Carol Thomas will demonstrate making a memorable journal and/or stationary art. Register by calling Teen Coordinator Amy Alessio at (847) 923-3191 or emailing aalessio@stdl.org. All participants must bring in an old pair of jeans to cut up for making the purse!

Teen Invasion Kickoff Barbecue

FRIDAY, JUNE 17 / NOON-3 P.M.
MAPLE PARK, NEXT TO THE SCHAUMBURG TOWNSHIP BUILDING AT ONE ILLINOIS BLVD., HOFFMAN ESTATES

Hosted by Schaumburg Township Youth and Family Services, this teen event will celebrate the beginning of summer and Teen Invasion. Teens from all over the township are invited to enjoy food, volleyball, Frisbee and softball. Attending the Barbecue counts as a ticket for the Teen Invasion program, too!

Teen Art Club

TUESDAYS, JUNE 28 & JULY 26
3:30-4:30 P.M.
YOUTH SERVICES CRAFT ROOM

Do you like to create art? Do you like to make crafts or paint? Then come join the Teen Art Club. Each month will feature a different theme or idea. Snacks and inspiration will be available. Students in grades 6-9 are welcome to participate. To register, call (847) 923-3191 or email aalessio@stdl.org. No fee!

Terror Tuesdays

EVERY TUESDAY IN JULY / 1-4 P.M.
TEEN CENTER AND AUDIOVISUAL DEPT.

Teens in grades 7-12 may drop by the Teen Center from 1-3 to enjoy board games, snacks, contests and prizes before heading over to the Audiovisual Department to view some horror movies.

Power Poetry

MONDAYS, JULY 11, 18, 25 / 7-8:30 P.M.
TEEN CENTER

Poetry is an art form. Teens in grades 7-12 can explore different forms of poetry during this three week workshop. Local author Catherine Stier will work with teens to share and craft their own expressions. Register by calling Teen Coordinator Amy Alessio at (847) 923-3191 or emailing aalessio@stdl.org.

Annual Road Rally

WEDNESDAY, JULY 13 / 7-8:30 P.M.
RASMUSSEN SOUTH (STARTING POINT)

Teams of 4 teens going into grades 7-12 will be invited to scour Towne Square for clues and treasure. An ice cream sundae bar and karaoke will be offered after the event. Register by calling Teen Coordinator Amy Alessio at (847) 923-3191 or emailing aalessio@stdl.org.

Teen Advisory Summer Board Meeting

TUESDAY, JULY 19 / 6-7 P.M.
RASMUSSEN SOUTH

The TAB plans and participates in programs throughout the Township all year. At the summer meeting we will be tasting favorite ethnic dishes from the area and voting on favorites. New members are always welcome. Interested teens going into grades 7-12 should call Amy Alessio at (847) 923-3191.

Teen Writing Club

TUESDAY, JULY 19 / 7-8:30 P.M.
RASMUSSEN SOUTH

Do you like to write stories or poems? Would you like to meet other people who like writing? Run by local author Catherine Stier, this growing group provides a chance for teens going into grades 7-12 to share stories, poems and tips on getting published.

Annual Mystery in the Library

WEDNESDAY, JULY 27 / 6:30 - 8:30 P.M.
RASMUSSEN SOUTH ROOM

Do you watch cop shows or like to read mysteries? Teens going into grades 7-12 can learn what detectives do to question witnesses and ferret out clues when a crime has been committed. Work with a team to solve a Mystery in the Library! Pizza and dessert will be served and prizes will be awarded to the team that solves the crime! A $5 fee is required for this event to secure your place, so register in person at the Adult Information Desk.

Knit Wits

TUESDAY, AUGUST 2 & THURSDAY, AUGUST 4
10 A.M.-NOON. / TEEN CENTER

Learn to knit like Julia Roberts and Sandra Bullock at this workshop. Each teen in grades 7-12 will learn the basics of casting on, knitting and purling as we make squares to create a blanket for a charitable organization. Basic supplies will be provided, but teens who know something about knitting are welcome to bring their own yarn or needles. Teens will also receive basic hat patterns. Register by calling Teen Coordinator Amy Alessio at (847) 923-3191 or emailing aalessio@stdl.org.

How to Draw Anime and Manga Art

WEDNESDAY, AUGUST 3 / 7-8 P.M.
RASMUSSEN SOUTH

Artist Shannon Krawetz will lead teens in grade the basics of anime and manga drawing styles. Register by calling Teen Coordinator Amy Alessio at (847) 923-3191 or emailing aalessio@stdl.org.

Teen Appreciation Week

AUGUST 8-14

All over Schaumburg Township, events will be held during this week to celebrate teens! At the library, teens going into grades 7-12 may pick up a coupon to clear $10 worth of fines (not fines for damaged materials) by inquiring at the Reader Services Desk of the central library or at the branch libraries.

Harry Potter Fest

TUESDAY, AUGUST 9 / NOON-4 (MOVIE THEN ACTIVITIES)
AUDIOVISUAL DEPARTMENT, THEN YOUTH SERVICES

Finish the new book Harry Potter and the Half-Blood Prince, then celebrate at the library! The movie of Harry Potter and the Prisoner of Azkaban will be shown in the back of the Audiovisual department from Noon-2:40 p.m., then go over to the Youth Services department to learn about secret writing, magical concoctions and hidden treasure! Snacks will be served. Young people ages 10 and up will be invited to this celebration of all things Harry Potter. Register at the Youth Services Information Desk.

SCHAUMBURG TOWNSHIP DISTRICT LIBRARY
130 SOUTH ROSELLE ROAD / SCHAUMBURG, IL 60193
(847) 985-4000 / WWW.STDL.ORG

This newsletter is written and produced bi-monthly.
Articles: Amy Alessio, Jean Dravet
Editing: Susan Miura   Graphics: Tom Javorcic

CONTRACT FOR TEEN VOLUNTEERS

Welcome! The library serves approximately 63,000 people every month. In order to keep services running smoothly in each department, it is important that volunteers and supervisors communicate clearly. Many of our volunteers have gone on to work at the library. To ensure that we establish a relationship of mutual understanding, please read the following contract and sign at the bottom.

1. I will come in at my designated dates and times to work, just as if this were paid employment.

2. I am responsible for completing my hours. If I am unable to come in at my designated time, I will call my supervisor and suggest times to make up the hours, pending his or her approval. In the case of illness or emergency, I will call as soon as I can and suggest dates for makeup. For example: *I can't make this week. Could I possibly come in for three hours for the next two weeks?*

3. I understand that I must do the assigned tasks at each shift, according to library staff direction. Staff try to vary the tasks to keep things more interesting, but there will be tasks that do not appeal, just as there may be in paid employment. The point of volunteer service is to help out in any way I can.

4. I understand that the library may terminate my volunteer participation if I do not cooperate with library rules and staff.

5. I understand that I will be sent home if I come in to work at a time when I am not expected. Because the library is open many hours, different shifts of staff work at different times. If I come in at a time when I am not expected, staff may not know me or have anything for me to do. This is disruptive to library work and will not be allowed.

6. I understand that I am expected to have a respectful attitude toward staff and patrons of the library at all times. If I have finished a project and staff are too busy to immediately direct me to another task, I will wait patiently until they are free.

7. I must wear my volunteer tag at all times when working at the library. All library staff do this for security reasons.

8. I will not search on the Internet or work on personal projects during my volunteer time.

Name:_____

Supervisor: _____

Date: _____

Phone Numbers: _____

TEEN INVASION 2005

June 13–August 13

TEEN INVASION 2005

June 13–August 13

SPONSORS

ALFRED CAMPANELLI YMCA

FRATERNAL ORDER OF POLICE, SCHAUMBURG LODGE #71

HOFFMAN ESTATES PARK DISTRICT

HOFFMAN ESTATES HIGH SCHOOL

JAMES B. CONANT HIGH SCHOOL

KEITH'S KOMIX

LASER QUEST

QDOBA MEXICAN GRILL

SCHAUMBURG HIGH SCHOOL

SCHAUMBURG PARK DISTRICT

SCHAUMBURG POLICE PATROL OFFICERS ASSOCIATION

SCHAUMBURG PRAIRIE CENTER FOR THE ARTS

SCHAUMBURG TEEN CENTER

SCHAUMBURG TOWNSHIP DISTRICT LIBRARY

SCHAUMBURG TOWNSHIP YOUTH AND FAMILY SERVICES

SCHAUMBURG TOWNSHIP DISTRICT LIBRARY
130 S. ROSELLE ROAD
SCHAUMBURG, IL 60193
(847)923-3191
WWW.STDL.ORG

June 13–August 13

Teens going into grades 7-12 can earn tickets this summer by going to museums or theaters, reading, taking a class, registering bicycles with the police department, volunteering and more. Each activity earns teens a number of tickets for drawings. Tickets can be turned in to the Reader Services Desk at the central library or at the Hoffman Estates or Hanover Park branch libraries. Other participating agencies may collect tickets as well.

Drawings will be held July 1, July 15, July 29, August 12. Prizes will include $50 and $25 gift certificates to area stores, free passes for local games, movie tickets and more! Each drawing is cumulative, so entering tickets early gives you more chances to win!

138

ACTIVITIES & POINTS

The following is a list of qualifying activities for Teen Invasion and how to prove that you participated in them. If an activity is worth more than one ticket, fill out the appropriate number.

VOLUNTEERING

2 TICKETS FOR 3 HOURS: You must volunteer for 3 hours at the Campanelli YMCA (this may not be divided). Have staff initial 2 tickets. Call Donald Langley at (847) 891-9622.

4 TICKETS FOR 6 HOURS: You must volunteer for all 6 hours at the Schaumburg Township Spectrum Youth and Family Services Center and have staff initial the tickets to receive 4. Call (847) 884-6212.

3 TICKETS PER EVENT: Volunteer at Schaumburg Park District's "Picnic in the Park," on either July 17 (Meineke) or August 7 (Volkening Lake). Contact Megan at the CRC (847) 490-7020.

1 TICKET PER 3 HOURS: Volunteer at another non-profit agency in the community, describe your experience, and have staff sign a ticket.

SPECIAL PLACES & EVENTS

1 TICKET: Attend the Kick-Off Barbecue! Friday, June 17, 12-3 p.m. in Maple Park, (next to) One Illinois Blvd. Have staff sign a ticket, and turn it in right at the event!

1 TICKET PER GAME: Attend a Flyers baseball game. Attach the stubs to the Teen Invasion drawing ticket.

---

1 TICKET PER VISIT: Visit the Schaumburg Teen Center (The Barn) at 231 S. Civic Dr. or attend a program there and have staff initial your ticket. Call Brianne at (847) 524-3388 for information and hours.

1 TICKET PER VISIT: Visit the Schaumburg Township or Vogelei Teen Centers or attend a program there and have staff initial your ticket. Call Julie Defalco at (847) 884-6213 for information and hours.

1 TICKET PER ACTIVITY: Attend a program through the Schaumburg or Hoffman Estates park districts, or the Township or Village of Schaumburg teen centers and have staff initial your tickets.

EXERCISING YOUR BRAIN

3 TICKETS PER VISIT: Go to a museum downtown or in the suburbs. Attach the stub or receipt to the Teen Invasion drawing tickets.

1 TICKET PER PERFORMANCE: Attend a performance at the Prairie Center for the Arts and attach the ticket stub to your Teen Invasion ticket.

2 TICKETS PER CLASS: Attend a summer school class through District 54 or 211 or a Harper College In-Zone class and have the teacher sign two tickets.

4 TICKETS: Complete the Schaumburg Township District Library Teen Summer Reading Program and have staff initial 4 tickets.

1 TICKET PER BOOK:
High School Students:
Read a book off of the high school required reading lists for your school, or off of a list of classics and write the title on your ticket.
Junior High School Students: Read a Young Readers' Choice Award book (available at the Schaumburg Twp. Dist. Library) and write the title on your ticket.

SUMMER FUN

1 TICKET PER 3 VISITS: Go to a pool in the area three times. Have lifeguards initial and date the ticket.

1 TICKET PER 4 MOVIES: Attach ticket stubs from 4 movies you've seen to a ticket.

1 TICKET: Register your bicycle with a local police department and list the number on your ticket.

3 TICKETS: Take a Schaumburg Park District teen trip to Navy Pier on August 12 and have your ticket signed by the trip supervisor.

2 TICKETS PER VISIT: Go to the Schaumburg Park District's "Sports Center" and use the batting tunnels during the week from 9 a.m.-6 p.m. Staple receipts from the $5 fee to your ticket.

WARM UP WITH A GOOD BOOK!

Goal: Read three books or listen to three audio books between January 1 and March 31. Write down the author, title, and a short review of the book. (Did you like it? Did you hate it? What was your favorite part?) Once you have completed your list return it to the library and enter your name in our drawing for prizes.

Last Name_____ First Name _____

Address_____ City_____ State _____ Zip_____

Age_____ School_____ Would you like to join our mailing list? (circle one)   Yes / No

BOOK 1

Title_____ Author _____

Liked it _____

Okay _____

Hated it _____

Review _____
_____
_____

BOOK 2

Title_____ Author _____

Liked it _____

Okay _____

Hated it _____

Review _____
_____
_____

BOOK 3

Title_____ Author _____

Liked it _____

Okay _____

Hated it _____

Review _____
_____
_____

POETRY CONTEST LETTER FOR NONWINNERS

Dear :

Thank you for entering our 6th Annual Teen Poetry Contest. This year over 50 entries were submitted, making the judging extremely difficult. Unfortunately, your poetry was not selected as a winner for this contest. But do not be discouraged! The caliber of the poetry submitted for the contest this year, including yours, was the best we have yet seen!

Judging of poetry is very subjective. For this contest, each person could enter twice, which is why our first- and second-place winners are the same person. Six teen volunteers and staff read all the poems and ranked their favorites numerically. Then the Teen Writing Club ranked the 11 finalists to score the winners. Final judges did not know the names of the poets, and no one who entered the contest had any part in the judging. We were looking for various criteria—unique or moving theme, unusual language or format, special effort such as researched details or use of iambic pentameter. You may not agree with the selections, and if the same poems had been sent to a different contest, the results may have been different. So please continue to write and to send your poetry to contests and to magazines for publication.

Two good books on getting published that are available at the library are *Children's Writer's and Illustrator's Market*, which has information on contests, publishers, and magazines for writers, and *The Young Writer's Guide to Getting Published*, by Kathy Henderson.

Also, try the website http://www.teenink.com, where you will find print and online publications completely written by young adults!

We also have a Teen Writing Club and summer programs on writing at the library, in addition to our four annual writing contests. We certainly hope to see you and your work again.

Sincerely,

Amy J. Alessio
Teen Coordinator

SLAY A BOOK

S	C	A	R	E
Any Book	Graphic Novel or 2 Magazines	Mystery/ Suspense	Teen Readers' Choice or Lincoln Award	Any Book
Horror or Fantasy	Any Book	Any Teen Library Program	Any Book	Realistic or Non-fiction
Any Book	Any Teen Library Program	SLAY a book Any Book	Any Teen Library Program	Horror or Fantasy
Realistic or Non-fiction	Any Book	Any Teen Library Program	Any Book	Graphic Novel or 2 Magazines
Any Book	Teen Readers' Choice or Lincoln Award	Graphic Novel or 2 Magazines	Award or Outstanding Book for College Bound	Any Book

Teen Summer Reading Program
SLAY A BOOK
2005

Name: _____

Phone:_____

Teens going into grades 7 – 12 can Slay a Book this summer and join in some spine-tingling events. The squares on the SCARE card indicate an activity or a genre of book. Participate in the reading program by picking up a SCARE (BINGO – type) card from the Reader Services Desk at the central library or at the Hoffman Estates or Hanover Park branch libraries. Fill out a review form when you read a book to enter additional weekly prize drawings during June and July. Finish the activities and/or books in a row of five squares to complete your SCARE card and pick up a prize between July 11 and August 31. Prizes will include Schaumburg Flyers game vouchers and more. Vouchers will be for the following dates: July 21, July 25, or August 3. Game vouchers will be given for completing a row of BINGO while supplies last, but everyone who finishes the program will receive a prize!

*Finishing the Summer Reading Program earns teens 3 tickets towards Teen Invasion! Call Amy Alessio Teen Coordinator, at (847) 923-3191 or email aalessio@stdl.org with questions.

SCHAUMBURG TOWNSHIP DISTRICT LIBRARY

Central Library
130 S. Roselle Road
Schaumburg, IL 60193
(847) 985-4000

http://www.stdl.org

Hanover Park Branch Library
1570 Irving Park Road
Hanover Park, IL 60133
(630) 372-7800

Hoffman Estates Branch Library
1550 Hassell Road
Hoffman Estates, IL 60195
(847) 885-3511

Chill Out and Read!

*Turn this in to the Reader Services Desk or the branch libraries to enter weekly raffles.

Chill Out and Read!

*Turn this in to the Reader Services Desk or the branch libraries to enter weekly raffles.

Phone: _____

Grade: _____

Name: _____

Title: _____
Author: _____
What did you think? _____
_____
_____
_____

Phone: _____

Grade: _____

Name: _____

Title: _____
Author: _____
What did you think? _____
_____
_____
_____

RINSING INSTRUCTIONS FOR TIE-DYEING

1. Put on gloves and old clothes and shoes. DO NOT LET THE WET GARMENT TOUCH ANYTHING UNTIL IT HAS BEEN RINSED AND DRIED. IT WILL STAIN EVERYTHING IT TOUCHES.

2. While the garment is still tied, rinse out as much dye as possible under warm running water or outside under a hose.

3. Gradually remove the rubber bands while still rinsing. Get out as much dye as possible.

4. Immediately wash the garment and ONLY the garment with hot water and a mild detergent. DO NOT WASH IT WITH A LOAD OF OTHER CLOTHES. THE COLORS MAY STILL BLEED AND RUIN ANYTHING THEY TOUCH.

5. Dry the garment by hanging it up or putting it in the clothes dryer.

6. Clean up your mess.

7. Stop by the library and show off your new creation!

BATTLE OF THE BANDS CONTRACT

_____ Library is pleased to provide your band/musical group with this opportunity to participate in our Battle of the Bands Contest. Bands will be signed up for available time slots on a FIRST-COME FIRST-SERVED basis only. We will not be able to save a specific time for anyone.

In order to make sure everything runs as smoothly as possible, please look over the following list of rules and obligations and discuss them with your band members. If you are in agreement, please sign and return this to

_____ [name], at the _____ Library, before _____ [date].

We will have a special "green room" set up to store your equipment. Please be prepared to have all of your band members present, all of your equipment set up, and all sound checks made 30 minutes before your scheduled per-

formance time. **If you are late or missing for ANY REASON, your band will forfeit its playing time.** Sorry, but we REALLY have to move things along smoothly.

The green room will be staffed by volunteer security personnel and ONLY BAND MEMBERS will be allowed in. NO EXCEPTIONS FOR ANY REASON!

Neither _____ Library nor any if its employees, agents, or volunteers will be held responsible for loss or damage to musical instruments, supplies, or other personal possessions.

Please contact _____ [name] at _____ [phone number] if you have any questions.

Schedule for the Evening

Time	Band Name	Contact Person	Phone Number
_____	_____	_____	_____
_____	_____	_____	_____
_____	_____	_____	_____
_____	_____	_____	_____

Please supply the names, signatures, and phone numbers of all band/group members.

Name	Signature	Phone Number
_____	_____	_____
_____	_____	_____
_____	_____	_____
_____	_____	_____
_____	_____	_____

LIBRARY SURVIVOR CLUES

L List of books to read (YA)
I It's art, and it's to sit on (YA)
B Books for teens (YA)
R Reference books for the older folks, but you'll find help here too
A Audio books for teens like you (YA)
R Reading a series like Buffy or Star Trek? Find all the latest titles circling around here (YA)
Y Young adults can find help here. The place to go when you have questions that need answers (YA)

S Special place for teens to hang out at the library (YA)
U Undeniably the coolest place to sit and listen to music CDs (YA)
R Reference material for teens (YA)
V Visible from the street, even at night, this sign defines the Zone (YA)
I Issues? We've got the information you need for all those "personal" questions (YA)
V Videos are found here
O Old issues are still around, Time, Rolling Stone . . . just go down
R Reference section for those smaller: encyclopedias, something about the author, and more

S SAT, PSAT, and ACT study guides and practice tests can be found here
K Killer CDs from all your favorite bands (YA)
I Interesting literature about interesting people for teens (YA)
L Looking for something to do? We have games you can check out and play here (YA)
L Look up information from how to spell a word to dates in U.S. history
S Stand in line (or sometimes not) to check out materials

W Where you go to look up books
I Internet access at your fingertips (YA)
N News about what's going on in the Zone (YA)
N Novels with colorful pictures (like comics) (YA)
E Exciting teen magazines to check out or browse through are located here (YA)
R Read the day's news from all over the country here

Booklists, bibliographies on the table
Art benches
Young adult area bookshelves
Adult reference
Young adult audio books
Young adult series racks
Young Adult Specialist Office

The Zone
Zone Listening Station
Young Adult Reference Section
Neon Zone sign
Young Adult "Got Issues?" and Information Pamphlet Display
Media Room
Periodicals
Children's Reference Section

Test Center
Young Adult CD Spinners
Young Adult Biographies
Game tub in the Young Adult Office
Homework shelf
Circulation desk

OPAC terminals
Young adult Internet stations
Zone newsletter display
Graphic Novels Section
Young Adult Magazine Section
Newspaper racks

CREATE A CREATURE CONTEST

Design any kind of creature you wish—anime, superhero, monster, whatever! Use a black, fine-point felt tip marker for your final entry and fill this form out completely. Your drawing must fit in the above space. Forms may be turned in to the Reader Services Desk of the central library or at the branch libraries by October 15. Teens in grades 7–12 may turn in up to three entries, but only one may win a prize. Entries will be displayed in the Teen Center during October and will be returned to artists upon request.

Name: _____

Grade: _____

Phone: _____

Name of Creature: _____

SCRIPT OUTLINE: WHO KILLED ANITA V. CATION?

Incident

Anita V. Cation, director of [name of your library], was found dead between the stacks of the magazine shelving at 10:00 A.M. on Wednesday, August 13, by maintenance man Bud Reddiholp. Subsequent examination of the scene by the police showed that Ms. Cation had been stabbed prior to being disposed of in the stacks, which led to a ruling of homicide.

Coroner's Report

A female body, later identified as Anita V. Cation, was found at approximately 10:00 A.M. on Wednesday, August 13, crushed in the magazine shelving stacks of the [name of your library]. Maintenance man Bud Reddiholp discovered the body after he was called to fix the stuck shelving. Marks on the floor indicated that a struggle had taken place. Autopsy revealed several stab wounds to the victim's chest, which were ruled the actual cause of death. The approximate time of death was between 9:15 and 9:45 A.M. that morning. A few dark drops were found on the carpeting outside the magazine room, but DNA test results have not yet been returned.

Report of Officer Evan Temper

Answered call about a body in the library at 10:02 A.M. The body of Anita V. Cation was lying in the stacks, crumpled. Maintenance man Bud Reddiholp called 911 after discovering the body, and he did a good job securing the area. He spotted dark splotches on the floor as mentioned in the coroner's report. I let forensics deal with those and turned over the body to make certain the victim was dead. Blood stains from several stab wounds were on the front of her shirt. When the detectives arrived, I helped other officers search the area and in the library's dishwasher found a knife that had been recently rinsed off. Forensics determined that it matched the wounds on the deceased.

Additional information about Officer Temper

- While Officer Temper was working on the crime area, Ivan Toklinup pestered him with questions and even took pictures of the body.

- Officer Temper is going to be promoted to detective next month.

- Officer Temper worked on a previous murder case at the library. He disliked the library director because she made fun of him for checking out the *Pocahontas* video. He recently bought a DVD player and checked out *Beauty and the Beast*. Ms. Cation threatened to take away the officer's library card because he constantly keeps DVDs out for more than the allotted three days.

- Officer Temper once arrested Cynthia Crystal, a former friend from high school, in the library parking lot for drunk driving. (She had crashed into the bike rack.) Cynthia offered him money to look the other way.

Suspects

Cynthia Crystal, a magazine clerk at [name of your library]

- Cynthia is the stepsister of Anita V. Cation, deceased.

- She is not very upset about her stepsister's death. There is a long-standing sibling rivalry between them. Cynthia had paid Anita's tuition for graduate school, and Anita was supposed to return the favor. However, when Cynthia was ready to go to graduate school, Anita claimed she could not afford it.

- Cynthia denies that Evan arrested her and instead says that he was stalking her and that she was not drunk. She will deny that Evan found an open beer bottle in her drink holder and his claim that she offered him money to look the other way.

- Cynthia has been heard to say that "cops are pigs."

- Her desk is near where the body was found, in the magazine shelving area.

- She was seen working in her stepsister's office at 9:00 A.M. on the day of the crime. The two were heard arguing, but Cynthia insists that Anita left the office at 9:15 A.M. to go get coffee.

- Cynthia says she stayed to search Anita's office for financial records, as she suspected that Anita had lots of money and could easily repay the tuition she owed Cynthia for graduate school. After Bud discovered the body and called the police, he immediately paged Cynthia, and she responded after five minutes, from Anita's office. She will say that she did not hear the page and that usually she is not important enough to be paged. When she arrived on the scene, she had a cup of coffee in her hand.

■ Cynthia may start crying if asked if she killed her stepsister. She will then ask the detective when Anita's will and finances will be processed.

Bud Reddiholp, maintenance man

■ Bud found the body. He was bringing up the mail when a library staff person asked him to come help, as the shelving was stuck. He opened the shelves, found the body, and immediately called 911 from a phone that would identify his location in the building.

■ Bud watches cop shows constantly and loves *CSI: Crime Scene Investigation.* He secured the area around the body after calling the police and looked for clues. He will refer to *CSI* and other TV shows frequently while being questioned.

■ He spotted some dark stains outside the room when he was waiting for Officer Temper to arrive.

■ He was seen wrapping a large piece of art down on the dock at 9:15 A.M. on the day of the crime. Soon after that, Alotta Dinero came into the garage. Bud likes Ms. Dinero and often helps her bring her library materials to her car. She offered him some choice vodka she had just bought, and they shared the bottle. Then he let her in the library and went to get the mail.

■ Bud wears an expensive watch.

■ Bud insists that he sells only used, discarded library materials to make a little extra cash, though he actually sells new library materials on e-Bay for a huge profit. Anita is in on this with him, and gets a percentage of the money.

■ Bud will plead the Fifth if asked whether or not Anita got money from the e-Bay transactions.

■ He will say that he donated some of the proceeds to the library in appreciation and that he knows nothing about Anita's finances.

Ivan Toklinup, ostensible head of [name of nearby branch library]

■ Ivan was seen pulling up to the library at 10:15 A.M. He questioned Officer Temper about the body while the officer was sealing off the crime area and even took pictures of the body. He tells people that he is just a very curious person.

■ Ivan says that he came over to the central library to get supplies.

■ He works late at the branch—from 8:30 A.M. to midnight some days. He explains his long hours only by saying that it is really busy over there.

■ He was seen wearing a shoulder holster. He says it discourages bad behavior at the branch.

■ Ivan will begin asking Detective Thommes questions during his interrogation and will compliment the detective on his investigation. Ivan will show his FBI badge and tell about the FBI safe house in the basement of the new branch.

■ Ivan will say that he has been investigating the ongoing theft of library furniture and was ready to make an arrest when he heard about Anita's murder on his police scanner.

Alotta Dinero, disgruntled wealthy patron and friend of the mayor

■ A stack of threatening letters from Alotta was found in Anita's office, complaining about poor service. Alotta will deny that there were more than ten or so and will insist that they were merely strongly worded.

■ She hates Anita, who once told her to get a life.

■ Alotta calls the desk three times a day with obscure questions. She will say that she likes to let the mayor know that citizens are getting their tax dollars' worth out of the library.

■ She mentions Mayor Carson in every sentence.

■ She will say that she was waiting in her car outside the library, talking on her cell phone, before the library opened. Her cell phone records do not confirm this.

■ Alotta was actually seen going into a supermarket around 9:00 A.M., where she purchased a bottle of expensive vodka "for a party." She then proceeded to the library, where she opened the vodka to sample it and spotted Bud on the garage dock, wrapping a large art object. Bud has been nice to her in the past, helping her bring her library materials to her car. He and she shared the vodka, then he let her into the library so she could get on a computer before anyone else arrived.

■ Alotta is running for a seat on the library board in hopes of hiring a better director, but she denies that she would ever actually kill Anita.

■ At this point in the questioning, she will threaten the detective's job and leave in a huff.

Ann Beans, library employee and famous horror author

■ Ann will begin by very sweetly offering Detective Thommes an autograph.

■ When asked why she works at the library if she writes world-famous best-sellers, she responds that it is to get ideas for new books and that people cannot begin to imagine what really goes on at the library.

■ When asked how she felt about Anita, Ann's first response is that she liked her. Eventually it will come out that Anita was once an editor who rejected twenty-seven of Ann's manuscripts, saying they were all "blood-filled nonsense."

■ Ann visits cemeteries to put herself in the mood to write. She once wore fangs and drank tomato juice constantly to get in character. She says she will do anything for research.

■ Ann was once suspended from work for a day for having a jar of poison in her locker. She will say there were bugs in the locker.

■ Anita would not give Ann vacation time to do author visits and would not stock her books, even after patrons asked for them. Ann denies this, even after seeing a memo from Anita to human resources declaring that Ann could not use vacation time for personal business activities. Ann will eventually admit that Anita thought that her books were silly and that she should focus her energy on writing quality literature.

■ On the morning of the crime, she went upstairs to get coffee and heard the stepsisters arguing. Ann actually listened outside the door, "to get dialogue ideas," and saw Anita leave and head toward the kitchen. Then Ann will say that she herself went to the kitchen for some coffee.

■ Ann likes to refer to her fans and how they "love her to death."

Malcolm Tenz, the cool teen librarian

■ Malcolm works in the little office in the Teen Center.

■ He tunneled out a secret back entrance, and when Detective Thommes asks about this, Malcolm will ask how he knows about it.

■ Anita put a camera outside Malcolm's door after someone complained that he was leaving the office in a cape and tights. He likes to do kids' programs at the hospital under the name of Captain Longjohns and is embarrassed about it. After Anita made fun of him and put up the camera, he was forced to make the secret back entrance. Anita also refused to let him leave early to put on his shows at the hospital.

■ When asked what he was doing at the time of the murder, Malcolm replies that was going to the kitchen to toast a bagel. He had forgotten his bagel and knife, and went back down to his office to get them.

■ He says that when he went back to his office at 9:30 A.M., he took a fifteen-minute phone call from his bank about unpaid credit card bills (for tunneling supplies). Then, when he went back up to the kitchen to eat his bagel and get coffee, he found another knife in the sink, covered with what looked like ketchup. He washed it off and put it in the library dishwasher, though he thought about taking it to add to his supplies for future teen programs.

■ Malcolm had a juvenile theft record that was supposed to be sealed, but Anita V. Cation kept referring to it in front of other people.

MYSTERY DINNER SOLUTION SHEET:
WHO KILLED ANITA V. CATION?

You will observe as a police detective interrogates six suspects in the murder of Anita V. Cation, the director of [name of your library]. Listen carefully and take notes in your dossier. After the detective's interrogation, the suspects will circulate from table to table to answer any further questions audience members may have. Write down your questions as soon as they occur to you so that you will be ready to interrogate the suspects yourself. Working as a team with the other teens at your table, discuss the interrogations and decide which suspect is the murderer. The first table to solve the crime and bring a completed solution sheet to the librarian wins. Only one solution sheet per table will be accepted.

Names of detectives

_____

_____

_____

_____

Time turned in _____

Who killed Anita V. Cation?

_____

_____

Why did he or she do it?

_____

_____

_____

_____

_____

_____

MYSTERY DINNER DOSSIER: WHO KILLED ANITA V. CATION?

Welcome to the Mystery Dinner. Your goal is to work with your tablemates to decide who killed the librarian Anita V. Cation and why he or she did it. Read the clues in this dossier carefully and pay close attention as the detective interrogates the six suspects. The first group of tablemates to submit a solution sheet that correctly identifies the murderer and the motive will win the game. Only one solution sheet per table is allowed.

Schedule

6:30 P.M.   Audience members arrive, enjoy dinner, and study their dossiers

6:50 P.M.   Host reviews the timeline for the evening and introduces the detective

6:55–7:40 P.M.   Questioning of suspects

7:45–8:10 P.M.   Ice cream bar open; teams deliberate while suspects individually travel from table to table to allow guests further questions

8:20 P.M.   All teams must turn in their answer sheets

8:25 P.M.   Killer is revealed and prizes are awarded to the winning team

Incident

Anita V. Cation, director of [name of your library], was found dead between the stacks of the magazine shelving at 10:00 A.M. on Wednesday, August 13, by maintenance man Bud Reddiholp. Subsequent examination of the scene by the police showed that Ms. Cation had been stabbed prior to being disposed of in the stacks, which led to a ruling of homicide.

Coroner's Report

A female body, later identified as Anita V. Cation, was found at approximately 10:00 A.M. on Wednesday, August 13, crushed in the magazine shelving stacks of the [name of your library]. Maintenance man Bud Reddiholp discovered the body after he was called to fix the stuck shelving. Marks on the floor indicated that a struggle had taken place. Autopsy revealed several stab wounds to the victim's chest, which were ruled the actual cause of death. The approximate time of death was between 9:15 and 9:45 A.M. that morning. A few dark drops were found on the carpeting outside the magazine room, but DNA test results have not yet been returned.

Officer Evan Temper, First Police Officer on the Scene

- Answered call about the body at 10:02 A.M.
- Is going to be promoted to detective next month
- Has worked on a previous murder case at the library
- Once arrested Cynthia Crystal, a former friend from high school, in the library parking lot for drunk driving

Suspects

Cynthia Crystal, a magazine clerk at [name of your library]

- Cynthia is the stepsister of Anita V. Cation, deceased.
- Her desk is near where the body was found, in the magazine shelving area.
- She was heard arguing with Anita that morning.

Bud Reddiholp, maintenance man

- Bud found the body. He spotted some dark stains outside the room when he was waiting for Officer Temper to arrive.
- He was seen wrapping a large piece of art down on the dock at 9:15 that morning. Soon after that, Alotta Dinero came into the garage.
- Bud will say that he sells only used, discarded library materials, but he wears an expensive watch.

Ivan Toklinup, ostensible head of [name of nearby branch library]

- Ivan was seen pulling up to the library at 10:15 A.M., and he questioned Officer Temper about the body while he was sealing off the area.

■ He works late at the branch—from 8:30 A.M. to midnight some days. He was seen wearing a shoulder holster.

Alotta Dinero, disgruntled wealthy patron and friend of the mayor

■ A stack of threatening letters from Alotta was found in Anita's office, complaining about poor service. She hates Anita, who once told her to get a life.

■ She calls the desk three times a day with obscure questions.

■ She was seen going into Dominick's around 9:00 A.M. After she purchased some vodka, she and Bud shared it in the library garage. Then he let her into the library even though it was not yet open to the public.

■ She is running for the library board in hopes of hiring a better director, but she denies that she would ever actually kill Anita.

Ann Beans, library employee and famous horror author

■ Anita was once an editor who rejected twenty-seven manuscripts from Ann, saying they were "blood-filled nonsense."

■ Ann visits cemeteries to put herself in the mood to write. She once wore fangs and drank tomato juice constantly to get in character.

■ Ann was once suspended from work for a day for having a jar of poison in her locker.

■ Anita would not give Ann vacation time to do author visits and would not stock her books, even after patrons asked for them. Anita thought Ann should write quality literature.

■ That morning, Ann went upstairs to get coffee and heard the stepsisters arguing. She was actually listening outside the door, "to get dialogue ideas."

Malcolm Tenz, the cool teen librarian

■ Malcolm works in the little office in the Teen Center.

■ Anita put a camera outside his door after someone complained that he was leaving in a cape and tights. He likes to do programs at the kids' hospital under the name of Captain Longjohns. After Anita put up the camera, he tunneled out a secret back entrance from his office.

■ At the time of the murder, Malcolm was going to the kitchen to toast a bagel, but he forgot his bagel and knife and had to go back down to his office to get them. He says he took a fifteen-minute call from the bank at 9:30 A.M.

■ After the call, he went back up to the kitchen, where he found another knife in the sink, covered with what looked like ketchup.

■ Malcolm had a juvenile theft record that was supposed to be sealed, but Anita V. Cation kept referring to it in front of other people.

Index

Amy J. Alessio is the Teen Coordinator at Schaumburg Township District Library in Illinois, where she creates and runs teen programs and coordinates the teen advisory board. She is the coeditor of YALSA's *Teen Read Week Manual*. Amy serves as a trainer in YALSA's Serving the Underserved program and has presented on teen and young adult service topics at state and national conferences.

Kimberly A. Patton is a young adult specialist at Lawrence Public Library in Kansas, where she runs teen programming as well as the young adult advisory board. Kim serves as a YALSA Serving the Underserved trainer and is an active speaker at state and national conferences.